GOVERNMENT PROCEDURES AND OPERATIONS

U.S. POSTAL SERVICE REFORM: ISSUES AND STRATEGIES

GOVERNMENT PROCEDURES AND OPERATIONS

Additional books in this series can be found on Nova's website under the Series tab.

Additional e-books in this series can be found on Nova's website under the e-book tab.

GOVERNMENT PROCEDURES AND OPERATIONS

U.S. POSTAL SERVICE REFORM: ISSUES AND STRATEGIES

MARTIN THOMAS
EDITOR

nova publishers
New York

Library of Congress Cataloging-in-Publication Data

ISBN: 978-1-53610-463-9

Published by Nova Science Publishers, Inc. † New York

CONTENTS

Preface		**vii**
Chapter 1	Reforming the U.S. Postal Service: Background and Issues for Congress *Michelle D. Christensen, Kathryn A. Francis and Garrett Hatch*	**1**
Chapter 2	U.S. Postal Service Workforce Size and Employment Categories, FY1995-FY2014 *Kathryn A. Francis*	**65**
Chapter 3	U.S. Postal Service Retiree Health Benefits and Pension Funding Issues *Kevin R. Kosar and Katelin P. Isaacs*	**85**
Chapter 4	U.S. Postal Service: Post Office Changes Suggest Cost Savings, but Improved Guidance, Data, and Analysis Can Inform Future Savings Efforts *United States Government Accountability Office*	**105**
Index		**145**

PREFACE

Congress designed the U.S. Postal Service (USPS) to be a self-supporting government agency. Since 1971, the agency has not relied upon annual appropriations to cover its operating costs. Rather, USPS has funded its operations mostly through the sales of postage and postal products and services. Since FY2007, however, the agency has run more than $40 billion in deficits and has reached its statutory borrowing limit. The agency does receive an annual appropriation of approximately $90 million per year, which amounts to about 0.1% of USPS's $65 billion operating budget. USPS's troubled financial condition has raised concerns about the viability of the agency. Many postal reform bills have been introduced in the 113th and 112th Congresses. These bills have proposed altering many aspects of postal operations, from raising the rates mailers pay to reducing the days of delivery and closing USPS post offices and mail sorting facilities. This book provides background information on the responsibilities, financial challenges and workforce issues facing the U.S. Postal Service (USPS). Additionally, it covers the current strategies and initiatives under development by the USPS and discusses further options for postal reforms.

In: U.S. Postal Service Reform
Editor: Martin Thomas
ISBN: 978-1-53610-463-9

Chapter 1

REFORMING THE U.S. POSTAL SERVICE: BACKGROUND AND ISSUES FOR CONGRESS*

Michelle D. Christensen, Kathryn A. Francis and Garrett Hatch

SUMMARY

This report provides background information on the responsibilities, financial challenges and workforce issues facing the U.S. Postal Service (USPS). Additionally, it covers the current strategies and initiatives under development by the USPS and discusses further options for postal reforms.

In FY2015, the USPS marked its ninth consecutive year of financial losses with a net loss of $5.1 billion. In addition, the USPS has reached its statutory debt limit of $15 billion. In recent years, the USPS has experienced growth in the package and shipping part of its business (known as Competitive Products). The USPS, however, has experienced sharp declines in both volume and revenue of its Market Dominant Products (e.g., First Class single-piece mail).

The USPS has struggled in recent years to fulfill its statutory obligation to prefund its health benefits liability for future postal retiree. Under a prefunding schedule established by the Postal Accountability and Enhancement Act, the USPS has made $20.9 billion in contributions since FY2007 but defaulted on its remaining $28.1 billion in payments. In

---

* This is an edited, reformatted and augmented version of a Congressional Research Service, Publication No. R44603, dated August 25, 2016.

its most recent financial statement, the USPS requested reforms that would integrate postal employee healthcare options with Medicare, thereby reducing costs and making the prefunding liability expense more manageable. Such reforms would require statutory authorization from Congress.

This report also covers several issues facing the USPS workforce. In recent years, initiatives designed to restructure the USPS retail and mail processing networks allowed the USPS to implement several workforce reduction strategies that helped cut costs. In FY2015, however, workforce costs increased. According to the USPS, this reversal was due to contract obligations and work hours associated with the growth in its labor-intensive package and shipping business.

Additional postal initiatives and reform options discussed in this report include (1) changes to postal delivery standards, (2) consolidation of mail processing facilities, (3) closure of retail post offices, (4) five-day delivery, (5) updates to the postal fleet, (6) nonpostal products and services; and (7) postal banking.

Appendix B of this report includes a table of House and Senate postal reform legislation introduced in the 113th and 114th Congresses, such as S. 2051, *Improving Postal Operations, Service, and Transparency Act of 2015* (iPOST Act) and H.R. 5714, *Postal Service Reform Act of 2016*.

For each bill, the table in **Appendix B** provides the bill number, title, sponsor, the committee(s) to which the bill was referred, a list of selected issues the bill covers, and the last major action (e.g., referral to committee, mark-up held).

OVERVIEW

Prior to enactment of the Postal Reorganization Act of 1970 (PRA),[1] mail delivery in the United States was the responsibility of the U.S. Post Office Department, a Cabinet-level department in the executive branch.[2] PRA reform efforts were driven largely by the view that the Post Office Department was ill equipped to meet the demands of the growing U.S. population and the changing economy.[3] Mail volume had risen sharply and the Post Office Department lacked the institutional flexibility to quickly respond to market changes.[4]

Today, the U.S. Postal Service (USPS or Postal Service) faces similar challenges but for different reasons. Between 2006 and 2015, total mail volume dropped sharply.[5] Market changes and global economic conditions contributed to the Postal Service's financial challenges and affected its efforts to control expenses and expand revenue.[6] Statutory mandates, such as the requirements to maintain six-day delivery and prefund health benefits for future retirees, may limit the actions USPS might take to mitigate these challenges. According to the Postal Service, "many of the structural reforms needed to ensure long-term financial viability, such as the resolution of our unsupportable [retiree health benefit] liability, can only be achieved with comprehensive legislation."[7]

FINANCIAL CHALLENGES FACING THE U.S. POSTAL SERVICE[8]

This section of the report covers the current financial responsibilities, challenges, and limitations facing USPS. These issues are the result of a confluence of factors including (1) the USPS's statutorily designed organizational and financial structure, (2) U.S. and global economic conditions over the past decade, and (3) the impact that technological innovations have had on the demand for postal products and services.

On the one hand, the USPS must sell enough postal products to maintain self-sufficiency and meet other statutory requirements, such as the retiree health benefit prefunding obligation. On the other hand, the USPS generally cannot expand its operations beyond the scope of postal products and services and other limited nonpostal products authorized by statute.[9] Statute also limits the USPS's ability to raise rates on certain postal products. These facts underlie many of the challenges facing the USPS and are also at the core of many of the reform efforts undertaken by the USPS and considered by Congress.

Financial Structure of the U.S. Postal Service

The current financial structure of the USPS was largely established by two statutes: the PRA and the Postal Accountability and Enhancement Act of 2006 (PAEA).[10] The PRA created the USPS, which replaced the U.S. Post Office Department, as an independent agency of the executive branch, responsible for generating enough revenue to finance its own operations. Prior to the PRA, the U.S. Post Office Department was a Cabinet-level agency and was not financially self-sustaining.

Since the passage of the PRA, the USPS has generated nearly all of its funding—about $69 billion in FY2015 according to the USPS's most recent financial report—by charging users of the mail for the costs of the services it provides.[11] Congress, however, does provide an annual appropriation—about $55 million in FY2016—to compensate the USPS for revenue it forgoes in providing free mailing privileges to the blind and certain overseas voters.[12] In addition, the annual appropriation compensates the USPS for debt it accumulated in the 1990s while providing postal services at below-cost rates to non-profit organizations.[13] Funds appropriated to the USPS for the annual reimbursement and revenue forgone are deposited in the Postal Service Fund, a revolving fund in the Treasury that consists largely of revenues generated from the sale of postal products and services.[14] The revenue in the Postal Service Fund is used to fund the operations of (1) the Postal Service, which includes the U.S. Postal Inspection Service (USPIS); (2) the U.S. Postal Service Office of Inspector General (USPSOIG); and (3) the Postal Regulatory Commission (PRC).[15]

Financial Condition of the U.S. Postal Service

The USPS's end-of-year financial results for FY2015 marked the ninth consecutive year of losses for the agency. In the years immediately prior to FY2007, the USPS ran modest profits. Between FY2007 and FY2015, the USPS accumulated $56.8 billion in financial losses, including a net loss of $5.1 billion in FY2015.[16] This trend was reversed in the first quarter of FY2016, which showed a net income of $300 million, compared to a net loss of $800 million at the same point in FY2015. The first quarter of FY2016 includes the holiday shipping season, which is one of the busiest times for USPS. The improvement in USPS's first quarter financial results are due in part to an increase in shipping and package volume and revenue as compared to the first quarter of FY2015. Additional factors, such as a temporary increase in select postal rates, known as a "temporary exigent surcharge" or "exigent increase," will be discussed in greater detail later in this section.

What Happens When USPS Ends the Year with a Net Loss?

Constituents may ask if the USPS receives appropriations, subsidies, or a "bailout" when it ends the fiscal year with a net financial loss. The USPS does not receive additional appropriations when it ends a fiscal year with a financial loss. The USPS does, however, benefit from access to debt instruments from the U.S. Treasury.

The USPS has statutory authority to borrow a maximum of $3 billion per fiscal year and hold a maximum total debt of $15 billion.[17] At the end of FY2012, the USPS reached its statutory debt limit. Further, USPS's total debt obligations have remained at $15 billion since FY2012.[18] As the USPS pays down its existing debt, it accumulates new debt up to its statutory maximum.[19] For example, on October 1, 2015, the USPS repaid $4 billion of its debt. It is expected, however, to borrow up to its statutory ceiling amount by the end of FY2016.[20]

USPS's $15 billion in debt is issued through a variety of loan instruments, which includes fixed and floating rate loans, an overnight credit line of $600 million, and a short-term credit line that allows the USPS to borrow up to $3.4 billion with two days prior notice.[21] The USPS's credit lines were fully drawn at the end of FY2015.[22]

Table 1. USPS Cash on Hand and Total Debt, FY2007-FY2015 (in millions)

	FY 2007	FY 2008	FY 2009	FY 2010	FY 2011	FY 2012	FY 2013	FY 2014	FY 2015
Cash Start FY	$997	$889	$1,432	$4,089	$966	$1,283	$2,086	$2,326	$4,906
Cash End FY	$889	$1,432	$4,089	$966	$1,283	$2,086	$2,326	$4,906	$6,634
Total Debt	$4,200	$7,200	$10,200	$12,000	$13,000	$15,000	$15,000	$15,000	$15,000

Source: U.S. Postal Regulatory Commission, Financial Analysis of United States Postal Service Financial Results and 10-K Statement, Fiscal Year 2015, March 29, 2016, p. 33 (Table II-20), at http://www.prc.gov/sites/default/files/reports/FY%202015%20 Financial%20Analysis%20Report.pdf.

Additionally, financial losses have caused the USPS to default on certain statutorily required payments, such as the retiree health benefit prefunding obligations.[23] Since FY2012, the USPS has defaulted on over $28 billion in statutorily required retiree health benefit prefunding obligations.[24] Use of debt instruments and default on certain retiree health prefunding payments has likely allowed the USPS to maintain cash-on-hand sufficient to cover its operational expenses throughout each fiscal year. As **Table 1** shows, the USPS has ended each fiscal year since FY2007 with at least $889 million cash-on-hand.

As shown in **Table 1** and **Figure 1**, in FY2015, the USPS had, on average, about 24 days[25] of operating cash-on-hand, sufficient to pay its day-to-day operating expenses, despite ending the year with $15 billion total debt outstanding. As of the end of FY2015, when all assets and liabilities are considered (including retirement accounts, health fund balances, cash and other assets), the USPS's total liabilities exceeded its assets by about $101 billion.[26]

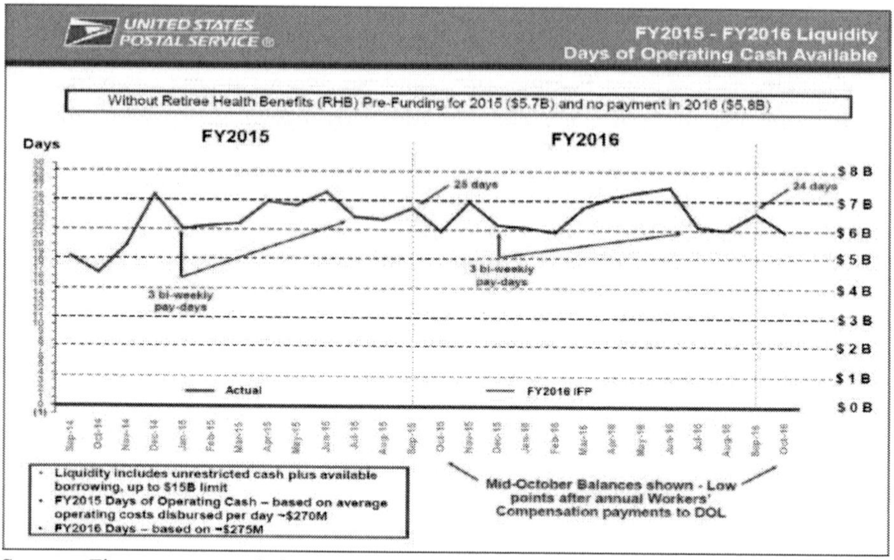

Source: Figure excerpted from U.S. Postal Service Board of Governors, *November 2015 Open Session Presentation*, p. 21.

Notes: *DOL* refers to the U.S. Department of Labor. FY2016 days of operating cash available estimates based on the U.S. Postal Service, *FY2016 Integrated Financial Plan (IFP)*, at http://about.usps.com/who-we-are/financials/ integrated-financial-plans/fy20 1 6.pdf.

Figure 1. USPS Days of Operating Cash, FY2015-FY2016.

Postal Services, Revenue, and Expenses

The PAEA, for the first time, provided a definition of the term *postal service*. Under the PAEA, postal service is defined as "the delivery of letters, printed matter, or mailable packages, including acceptance, collection, sorting, transportation, or other functions ancillary thereto."[2] This definition is significant because it prevents the Postal Service from developing new nonpostal products (e.g., expanded banking and financial services) that could compete with private industry.[28]

The PAEA also changed how postal rates are established and divided postal products into two distinct groups: market dominant products and competitive products.[29]

Market Dominant and Competitive Products	
Market dominant products are those in which the USPS is considered to have a monopoly over the service, such as first-class mail or standard mail (i.e., advertising mail). Competitive products, such as shipping and packages services, are those in which the USPS competes with the other companies in the private market (e.g., Fed Ex, UPS).	
Market Dominant Products include:	**Competitive Products include:**
First-Class Mail	Priority Mail@
Standard Mail	Priority Mail Express@
Periodicals	Parcel Select@
Post Office Box Services	International Priority Airmail@

Prior to the passage of the PAEA, there was concern that the USPS was using its revenue from market dominant products to subsidize the costs of competitive products. Cross-subsidization could, potentially, provide an advantage for the USPS in the competitive market by creating artificially low prices that did not include all the costs attributable to those products. The PAEA addressed this issue by forbidding the subsidization of competitive products with market dominant revenue and establishing the Competitive Products Fund (CPF), which receives deposits from the Postal Service Fund for revenues derived from the sale of competitive products.[30]

Postal Revenue

In FY2015, overall revenue from postal products and services was $68.951 billion, which was an increase of $1.097 billion (or 1.6%) from FY2014. The increase was due in large part to revenue from competitive products, which offset decreased revenue from market dominant products.

Nevertheless, revenue generated from the sale of market dominant products accounts for approximately 74% of USPS's annual operating revenue.[31]

As shown in **Figure 2**, total revenue from market dominant products was $52.426 billion in FY2015, a decrease of approximately $340 million (or

0.64%) from FY2014. Total revenue from competitive products, however, was approximately $16.52 billion in FY2015, an increase of $1.437 billion (or 9.52%) from FY2014.

Within the market dominant category, standard mail (i.e., advertising mail) remained one of the few profitable products. Revenue from standard mail increased approximately $217 million (or 1.24%) from FY2014 to FY2015.[32]

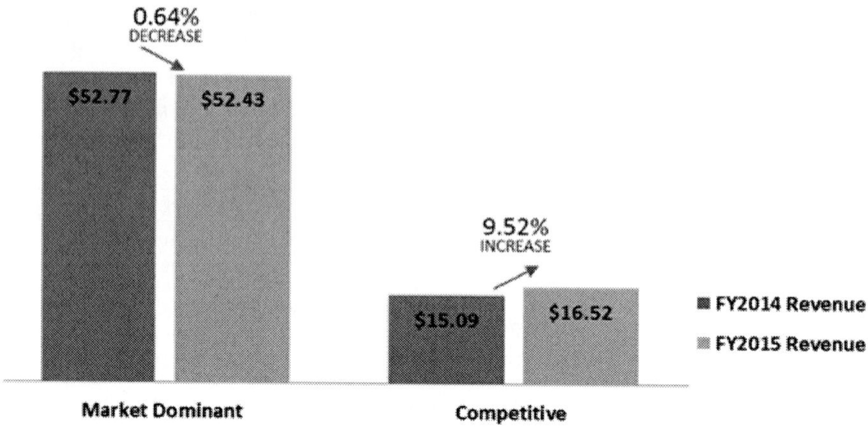

Source: U.S. Postal Service, *Final Revenue, Pieces, and Weight by Classes of Mail and Special Services for Fiscal Year 2015*, October 2015, at http://about.usps.com/who-we-are/financials/revenue-pieces-weight-reports/fy2015- q4.csv.

Figure 2. USPS Revenue, by Mail Category; FY2014 and FY2015, in billions.

Historically, competitive products have constituted a much smaller share of USPS revenue than market dominant products. Competitive products account for a larger proportion of USPS revenue than they do of USPS volume. For example, in FY2015, competitive products represented approximately 3% of mail volume, but they accounted for approximately 24% of USPS revenue. See **Figure 3** below.

While market dominant products made up 97% of USPS's FY2015 volume, they generated less revenue per piece ($0.35) than competitive products ($4.17).[33]

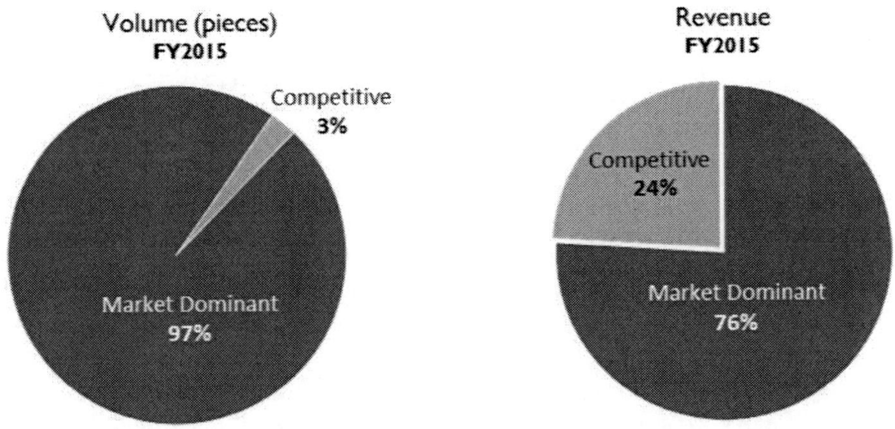

Source: U.S. Postal Service, *Final Revenue, Pieces, and Weight by Classes of Mail and Special Services for Fiscal Year 2015*, October 2015, at http://about.usps.com/who-we-are/financials/revenue-pieces-weight-reports/fy2015- q4.csv.

Figure 3. USPS Products' Contribution to Volume and Revenue; Market Dominant and Competitive.

As explained by the USPS, since competitive products are a relatively small percentage of total mail volume, future growth in shipping and packages might not offset future decline in market dominant products:

> Because Shipping and Packages represents only 20.3% of our 2014 operating revenue, compared to First-Class and Standard Mail, which represents 67.5% of operating revenue, revenue growth in Shipping and Packages, by itself, cannot fully offset the declines in First-Class Mail. Furthermore, the profit margins on both First-Class Mail and Standard Mail are greater than that of Shipping and Packages. As a result, revenue from Shipping and Packages would have to grow at a substantially higher rate than the decline in First-Class Mail revenue in order to replace the lost profit contribution of First-Class Mail.[34]

Furthermore, the processing and delivery costs for competitive products, such as First-Class Package Service or Priority Mail, are greater than those of most market dominant products. For this reason, USPS's competitive products might be sold at a lower margin than their market dominant counterparts, meaning that a lower percentage of competitive product revenue is retained as profits for the USPS.[35]

Mail Volume

In FY2015, mail volume for market dominant products dropped by 1.9 billion pieces, which is approximately 1.3% below FY2014. The decline for certain market dominant products was more pronounced than others. For example, in FY2015, first-class single-piece mail, a market dominant product that has historically been the largest source of revenue for the USPS, saw volume drop by nearly 1.4 billion pieces, or 2.1%.

In contrast, competitive mail volume, which is primarily shipping and package services, increased by more than 556 million pieces. This increase represents growth of 16.4% from FY2014.

Figure 4 shows the mail volume for market dominant and competitive products for FY2014 and FY2015. Detailed information on USPS's revenue and volume for FY2014 and FY2015 is provided in **Appendix A**.

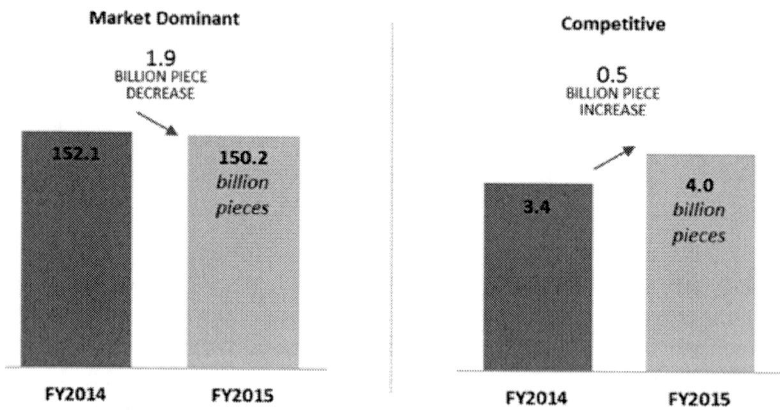

Source: U.S. Postal Service, *Final Revenue, Pieces, and Weight by Classes of Mail and Special Services for Fiscal Year 2015*, October 2015, at http://about.usps.com/who-we-are/financials/revenue-pieces-weight-reports/fy2015- q4.csv.

Figure 4. Market Dominant and Competitive Mail Volume, FY2014-FY2015; In billions.

Long-Term Trends

Total mail volume and revenue have been consistent or in decline for the past 10 years. Periods of decline have been driven largely by reductions in market dominant mail volume and revenue, which have dropped sharply since FY2009.[36] The decline in market dominant volume has been driven by a variety of economic factors and long-term market trends, such as transition to electronic mail, that have altered the public's use of the postal service for more than a decade.

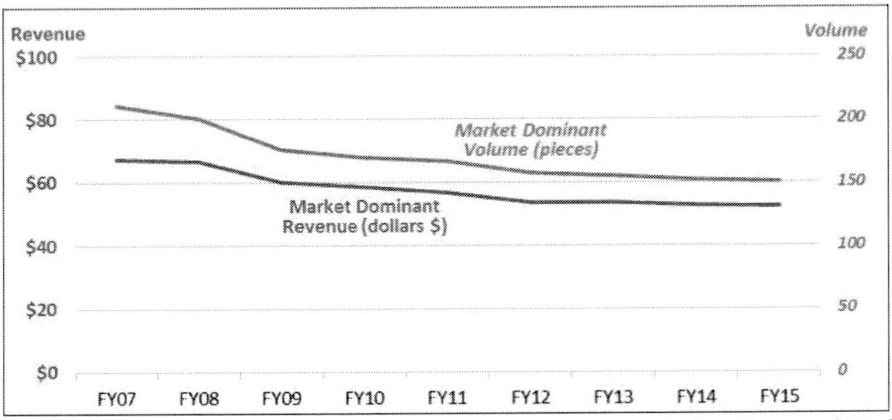

Sources: U.S. Postal Service, *Final Revenue, Pieces, and Weight by Classes of Mail and Special Services for Fiscal Year 2015*, October 2015, at http://about.usps.com/who-we-are/financials/revenue-pieces-weight-reports/fy2015- q4.csv. Figure created by CRS using data from U.S. Postal Service "Decade of Facts and Figures," at http://about.usps.com/who-we-are/postal-facts/decade-of-facts-and-figures.htm.

Figure 5. Market Dominant Revenue and Volume, FY2007-FY2015; In billions.

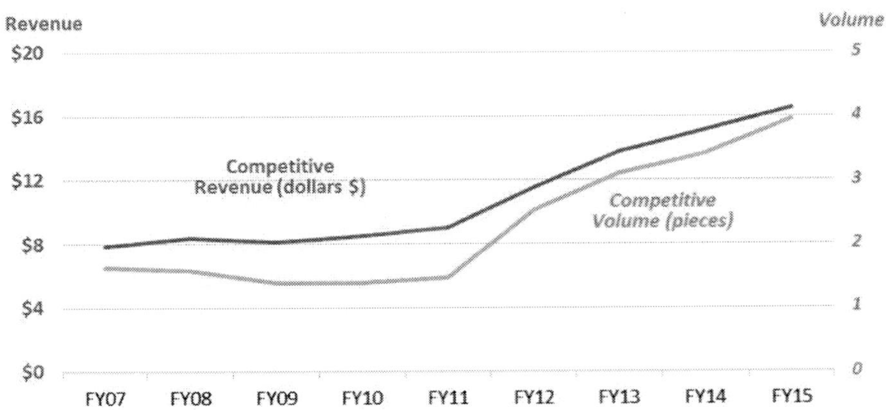

Sources: See Figure 5.

Figure 6. Competitive Revenue and Volume, FY2007-FY2015; In billions.

As shown in **Figure 6**, growth in both competitive product volume and revenue has likely offset some of the revenue lost from the continued decline in market dominant products. **Figure 7** below shows USPS's total annual mail volume and operating revenue for FY2005 through FY2015.

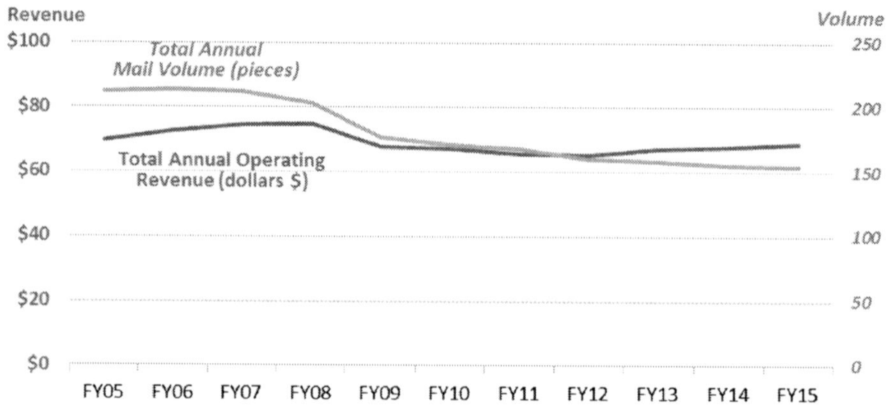

Sources: U.S. Postal Service, *Final Revenue, Pieces, and Weight by Classes of Mail and Special Services for Fiscal Year 2015*, October 2015, at http://about.usps.com/who-we-are/financials/revenue-pieces-weight-reports/fy2015- q4.csv. Figure created by CRS using data from U.S. Postal Service "Decade of Facts and Figures," at http://about.usps.com/who-we-are/postal-facts/decade-of-facts-and-figures.htm.

Figure 7. Total USPS Mail Volume and Revenue, FY2005-FY2015; In billions.

From FY2005 to FY2015, total annual mail volume dropped 57.5 billion pieces. The drop was largely due to volume lost in market dominant products. Total annual operating revenue, however, has remained relatively flat over the past decade. The figure shows the sharp declines in revenue and volume, which were likely due to the economic recession. While total annual volume remained in decline after FY2012, total annual revenue began to recover. By FY2015, total annual revenue was $68.9 billion, or $1 billion below what it had been in FY2005. Additionally, in FY2014 and FY2015, total annual revenue included a temporary increase in market dominant prices.[37]

Exigent Price Increase

Under the PAEA, price increases for market dominant products are limited to a formula based on annual, unadjusted changes in the Consumer Price Index for Urban Customers (CPI-U).[38] During "extraordinary or exceptional" circumstances (a term not defined in statute or regulation),[39] the PAEA allows the USPS to petition the PRC for an expedited postal rate adjustment. This exigent surcharge is a rate increase above what USPS would otherwise receive based on the CPI-U formula.

In July 2010, the USPS made its first request to the PRC for an exigent surcharge.[40] In its 2010 exigent request, the USPS sought to increase rates on its market dominant products by approximately 5.6% due to poor economic conditions and decreased mail volume. The "extraordinary or exceptional" circumstance, according to USPS's request, was the "unprecedented drop in mail volume," which they argue was caused by the recession.[41] The PRC denied USPS's request, in part because PRC found that multiple factors contributed to reduced mail volume, not all of which were due to the recession.[42]

In 2013, the USPS filed and the PRC approved a rate increase of 4.3% on market dominant products.[43] Pursuant to the PRC's order, the increase went into effect on January 26, 2014.[44] Originally, the increase was only to be in effect until the USPS recovered an additional $2.8 billion in lost revenue, which was the amount the PRC determined to be attributable to the recession.[45] At the time, the temporary increase was expected to be in place for less than two years.[46]

The exigent price increase has allowed the USPS to hold revenue for market dominant products steady, despite continued losses in volume. The USPS challenged the PRC methodology in court, arguing that the increase should be permitted to continue indefinitely. On June 5, 2015, the DC Circuit Court delivered an opinion upholding the temporary nature of the increase. This opinion, however, stated that the one aspect of the PRC methodology for calculating the cumulative losses attributable to the recession was "arbitrary and capricious" and must be revisited to resolve disagreement with the methodology proposed by the USPS.[47] Following the ruling of the DC Circuit Court, the PRC increased the amount that the USPS could collect in exigent price revenue by an additional $1.4 billion.[48]

On February 25, 2016, the PRC issued a "Notice of the Removal of the Exigent Surcharge," which announced the Postal Service's plan to remove the surcharge on April 10, 2016.[49] As of April 10, rates on many market dominant products and services have dropped to the price they were prior to the exigent surcharge.[50] For example, the price of a First-Class Forever stamp dropped from $0.49 to $0.47, and the price of an International Forever stamp dropped from $1.20 to $1.15.[51] Rates for select products and services used largely by bulk mailers (e.g., discounted rates for presorted mail) were adjusted using additional criteria.[52]

The exigent surcharge had been in place since January 26, 2014. **Table 2** shows the estimated revenue from the exigent surcharge for FY2014 and FY2015.

Table 2. Estimated USPS Revenue from Exigent Surcharge, FY2014-FY2015 (in billions)

	FY2014	FY2015
Revenue (excluding exigent surcharge)	$66.4	$66.8
Revenue from exigent surcharge	**$1.4**	**$2.1**
Total Revenue	$67.8	$68.9
Operating Expenses	$66.4	$67.7
Income/Profit (with exigent surcharge)	$1.4	$1.2
Income/Profit/Loss (excluding exigent surcharge)	**$0.0**	**-$0.9**

Sources: U.S. Postal Service, *2015 Report on Form 10-K*, pp. 13-16; also see U.S. Postal Service Board of Governors, *November 2015 Open Session Presentation*.

Note: *Operating Expenses* excludes certain retiree and workers' compensation costs.

In FY2014 and FY2015, the estimated revenue from the temporary exigent surcharge was $1.4 billion and $2.1 billion, respectively. Total revenue (excluding the surcharge) was $66.4 billion in FY2014 and $66.8 billion in FY2015. In the two full years that the exigent surcharge has been in place, it has contributed an estimated 2.1% and 3.2% to the total revenue of the USPS (or an estimated 2.7% and 4.0% to the total market dominant revenue, respectively).

Expenses from Operations

To address its financial challenges, the USPS has made several operational adjustments intended to align its revenue, mail volume, and operating expenses, [53] including

- changes to its workforce (e.g., increased use of non-career employees);
- consolidation of delivery routes and reductions in number of delivery facilities;
- reductions to retail office hours; and
- realignment of its mail processing and distribution network.[54]

For FY2015, USPS's operating expenses were about $67.7 billion. **Table 3** provides a further breakdown of expenses for FY2014 and FY2015.

Table 3. USPS Operating Expenses, FY20 1 4-FY20 15 (in billions)

	FY2014	FY2015	Change	Chg (%)
Salaries/Compensation	$35.113	$35.931	$0.818	2.330%
Health benefits –current employees	$4.804	$4.774	-$0.030	-0.624%
Workers' compensation	$1.372	$1.452	$0.080	5.831%
Retirement	$5.758	$6.239	$0.481	8.354%
Retiree health benefits –current year premiums (not prefunding payments)	$2.985	$3.111	$0.126	4.221%
Other personnel related expenses	$0.326	$0.334	$0.008	2.454%
Total Personnel-Related Operating Expenses	**$50.358**	**$51.841**	**$1.483**	**2.945%**
Transportation (e.g., air and highway transportation contracts)	$6.600	$6.600	$0.000	0.000%
Depreciation costs	$1.800	$1.800	$0.000	0.000%
Supplies and services	$2.600	$2.700	$0.100	3.846%
Rent, utilities, and other expenses	$5.000	$4.800	-$0.200	-4.000%
Total Operating Expenses	**$66.358**	**$67.741**	**$1.383**	**2.084%**

Sources: U.S. Postal Regulatory Commission, Financial Analysis of United States Postal Service Financial Results and 10-K Statement, Fiscal Year 2015, March 29, 2016, pp. 11-12; U.S. Postal Service Board of Governors, November 2015 Open Session Presentation.

Each fiscal year, roughly two-thirds of the USPS's operating expenses are attributable to personnel costs, through salaries, compensation benefits, workers' compensation and retiree benefits—excluding the retiree health prefunding payments.[55] For FY2015, personnel-related expenses were $51.8 billion, an increase of $1.5 billion (or 2.9%) from FY2014.[56] The largest line-item for personnel costs is salaries.[57] From FY2010 to FY2014 the costs for salaries and other compensation decreased steadily. USPS spent $35.1 billion on these costs in FY2014 and $37.5 billion in FY2010, with expenditures dropping an average of $600 million each year.[58] These reductions have been driven by a number of USPS management decisions, including the use of voluntary separation incentives and the increased reliance on non-career employees. The current labor and employment challenges of the USPS are discussed in greater detail in the "Current Issues Facing the USPS Workforce" section of this report.

This trend, however, reversed in FY2015 when USPS's salaries and compensation costs increased by 2.3% to $35.9 billion. The USPS attributes the increased costs to "contractually obligated salary escalations and additional work hours associated in part with the growth in the more labor-intensive Shipping and Packages business."[59]

The USPS has not seen significant reductions in non-personnel costs in recent years. For the period from FY2010-FY2015, total non-personnel related expenses have been about $15 to $16 billion annually.[60] The largest non-personnel expenses are transportation costs. The USPS spent $6.6 billion for transportation in FY2015, largely on contracts for air, ground, and water transportation of the U.S. mail.[61] Fuel expenses are also included under *transportation,* but they contribute a relatively small portion of costs. The other non-personnel expenses for FY2015 include supplies and services ($2.7 billion), rent and utilities ($4.8 billion), and depreciation of USPS assets ($1.8 billion).

While the USPS has control over the majority of its expenses, there are expenses mandated by law, including the RHBF prefunding requirement. Additionally, the USPS reached its statutory debt limit of $15 billion[62] in FY2012 and as a result the USPS has no remaining flexibility to finance operations or respond to market changes through borrowing without further action from Congress.[63]

Prefunding Requirement for Retiree Health Benefits[64]

The PAEA requires the USPS to prefund its retiree health benefits.[65] To accomplish this task, the PAEA established a prefunding schedule beginning in FY2007. For the first 10 years (FY2007 FY2016), the USPS is to make statutorily prescribed prefunding payments into the Postal Service Retiree Health Benefits Fund (RHBF). The RHBF was created under the PAEA as an on-budget account in the U.S. Treasury. The statutorily prescribed prefunding payments range from $5.4 billion to $5.8 billion annually.

The statutorily prescribed payments conclude in FY2016. Beginning in FY2017, the USPS is to continue to make annual payments to the RHBF in amounts determined by OPM. Per the PAEA, OPM is to, on an annual basis, compute the difference between the size of current employees' future retiree healthcare benefit liability and the current RHBF balance, and then determine a schedule of annual payments to liquidate any outstanding liability by September 30, 2056.

Pursuant to the PAEA, the USPS payments to the RHBF are to be derived from operating revenue held in the Postal Service Fund. Beginning in FY2017, the USPS may begin accessing funds from the RHBF to pay for its current retirees' health benefits.

Since the prefunding payment schedule began in FY2007, the USPS has made three of its annual payments in full—FY2007, FY2008, and FY2010. Congress reduced the FY2009 payment owed from $5.4 billion to $1.4 billion, which the USPS paid. The USPS defaulted on each of its annual payments for FY2011 through FY2015.[66] The FY2016 payment is due September 30, 2016.[67] In total, through FY2015 the USPS has contributed $20.9 billion to the RHBF and has defaulted on payments totaling $28.1 billion.[68]

The prefunding policy has been a contentious issue. Arguments advanced in favor of the policy center on the policy protecting future customers of the USPS and taxpayers by ensuring that they will not need to finance retirement benefits currently incurred by the USPS. However, according to the USPS, the prefunding requirement has contributed "significantly" to its financial losses.[69] In its most recent financial statement, the USPS reiterated its pursuit of legislation that would allow the USPS to change how it offers health insurance to its employees and retirees. The USPS argues that such changes would "eliminate any necessity for the [RHBF] prefunding requirement...."[70] The changes would require statutory authorization from Congress.

CURRENT ISSUES FACING THE USPS WORKFORCE[71]

USPS's challenging financial circumstances have prompted the agency to implement several cost-cutting strategies, one of which has been to reduce the size and cost of the USPS workforce. The sections below discuss three USPS initiatives to reduce its workforce size and cost: (1) attrition and separation incentives, (2) increased use of non-career employees, and (3) non-personnel initiatives that could impact workforce size and cost. The sections focus on implementation of these three initiatives since FY2007, at which time the USPS began to experience substantial revenue losses.

Size and Cost of the USPS Workforce

The USPS has reduced its workforce size through voluntary attrition and separation incentives.[72] The total number of USPS employees declined 21%

(168,052 employees) between FY2007 and FY2014, from 785,929 to 617,877.[73] To increase the voluntary attrition rate, the USPS has offered certain employees separation incentives to resign or retire early, which have ranged from $10,000 to $20,000 per person.[74] Between FY2007 and FY2014, 55,473 employees accepted a separation incentive (**Table 4**). Many of the separation incentives offered between FY2012 and FY2014 were associated with various postal facility closure initiatives, which are discussed later in this report.[75]

Table 4. Total Number of Separated USPS Career Employees, FY2007-FY2014

Fiscal year	Total number of separations	Total numberof employees separated *withoutan* incentive	Total number of employees separated *withan* incentive	Incentive amount (per person)	Target employee category	Total cost of incentive(millions)
2007	7,437	7,437	0	0	N/A	0
2008	33,685	33,685	0	0	N/A	0
2009	42,235	42,235	0	0	N/A	0
2010	40,873	20,073	20,800	$15,000	APWU employees; mail handlers	$312.0
2011	30,302	28,058	2,244	$20,000	Administrative employees	$44.9
2012	33,137	25,920	4,192	$20,000	Postmasters	$129.2
			3,025	$15,000	Mail handlers	
2013	41,823	17,991	22,609	$15,000	APWU employees	$339.1
			1,223	0	Managers, supervisors, postmasters	
2014	28,900	27,520	1,380	$10,000	Postmasters	$13.8
Total	258,392	202,919	55,473	N/A	N/A	$839.0

Source: Adapted from Table 1 found at GAO, *U.S. Postal Service, Status of Workforce Reductions and Related Planning Efforts*, GAO-15-43, November 13, 2014, p. 12, at http://www.gao.gov/assets/670/666884.pdf; CRS analysis of data from "Form 10-Ks"; data provided by USPS staff on June 8, 2015.

Notes: FY2007 data may be incomplete, as USPS only had partial access to data due to the agency's migration from its legacy human resources system to its current system during that year. The total number of separated employees is not equal to the total reduction in the number of employees between FY2007 and FY2014. The difference might be due to additional hiring for existing or newly created positions that occurred over that time period.

The USPS has utilized separation incentives to avoid reductions in force (RIFs), which involve involuntary employee layoffs upon the abolishment of agency positions.[76] On January 9, 2015, however, the USPS implemented a RIF for 249 postmasters who did not accept a separation incentive offered in FY2014.[77] Of the 249 postmasters subject to the RIF, 169 opted for a Discontinued Service Retirement (DSR), and the remaining 80 who were not eligible for DSR received severance pay based on their age and years of service. According to the USPS, all postmasters affected by the RIF were offered part-time career positions at the USPS.[78]

Increased Use of Non-Career Employees

The USPS categorizes its workforce into two employee types: career and non-career. Career employees serve in permanent positions and are typically provided full federal benefits.[79] Non- career employees, in contrast, serve in time-limited or otherwise temporary positions. In many cases, non-career employees earn lower wages and are not provided benefits that are provided to career employees. For example, non-career employees are not eligible for federal life insurance and are not covered under the Federal Employees Retirement System (FERS).[80]

The USPS has increased its use of non-career employees in an effort to contain costs. The number of non-career employees grew by 28% between FY2007 and FY2014, from 101,167 to 129,577.

The number of career employees, in contrast, decreased by 28% over the same time period, from 684,762 to 488,300. The largest increase in the number of non-career employees occurred between FY2011 and FY2014, rising by 46.1% (40,878 employees).[81] The influx of non-career employees during that period was primarily attributable to the establishment of three new non-career positions: Postal Support Employees (PSEs), City Carrier Assistants (CCAs), and Mail Handler Assistants (MHAs).[82] Employees in these three positions constituted 51% of the USPS non-career workforce in FY2014.[83]

According to the USPS, non-career employees can reduce the overall costs of certain agency functions.[84] Non-career employees can often perform the full range of duties undertaken by their career counterparts at lower wage rates. For instance, non-career CCAs can perform the duties of career city letter carriers at a starting rate of $15.00 per hour versus $16.71 per hour.[85] The wage difference between CCAs and city letter carriers is greater after accounting for benefits and overtime ($19.35 per hour versus $46.11 per hour, respectively), according to a 2014 Government Accountability Office (GAO) report. In addition, the USPS OIG reported that non-career employees could be used in place of career employees earning overtime and thus could reduce compensation costs.[86]

Impact of USPS Workforce Initiatives on Costs

The USPS's initiatives to reduce the size and cost of its workforce have reportedly contributed to lowered compensation expenses in recent years. The USPS's total compensation costs decreased $526 million from FY2013 to FY2014, and the PRC found that 36.1% of the decreased amount ($190 million) resulted from increased use of non-career employees and a decrease in employee work hours.[87] For instance, the PRC reported that increased use of CCAs and MHAs, combined with the reduction in their career counterparts, reduced the productive hourly wage rate for the mailhandling and city carrier functions by 3.5% and 5.4%, respectively, from FY2013 to FY2014.[88] The remaining 63.9% of the reduced amount ($336 million) reflected a one-time cost of separation incentives that were paid in FY2013, according to a 2015 PRC report.[89] Similarly, a 2016 USPS OIG report asserted that the decline in work hours over time—a 2.8% average decline per year between 2006 and 2015—has translated into cost savings.[90]

A 2014 GAO report on the USPS workforce, however, found that the USPS's *overall* expenses did not decrease amid the agency's efforts to reduce workforce size and work hours.[91] According to the report, USPS's total expenses did not decline alongside reduced workforce size and work hours from FY2006 to FY2014 and instead fluctuated over the eight-year period.[92] The report attributed the fluctuation to required annual RHBF payments, which varied by year.[93] The USPS's overall expenses still declined at a slower rate compared to employee work hours (7.1% versus 24%, respectively) when excluding RHBF payments, according to the report. In response to the GAO report, the USPS attributed the slower rate of decline in overall expenses to increased hourly wage and benefit costs, increased non-personnel expenses, and other fixed costs that do not decline with decreases in mail volume.[94]

U.S. Postal Service's Current Strategies and Initiatives

This section provides information on the U.S. Postal Service's current five-year business plan and several ongoing USPS reform initiatives. The reform initiatives discussed in this section cover a wide range of issues and various aspects of postal operations. In many instances, these initiatives are underway, pursuant to the USPS's current legal authorities. Continuation of these initiatives does not require legislative action by Congress. In some cases, however, Congress has proposed legislation that would halt or amend actions that the USPS has already initiated.

U.S. Postal Service's Five-Year Business Plan[95]

The USPS's *Five-Year Business Plan* (hereinafter, USPS *Business Plan*) provides detailed analyses of the short- and long-term financial situation of the USPS and includes several reform proposals that the Postal Service argues would help it progress toward financial stability and long-term sustainability.[96] Many of the proposed initiatives involve further adjustments to postal delivery networks. In its *Business Plan*, the USPS argues the adjustments—which include the closure and consolidation of selected mail processing facilities—are necessary to improve efficiency and address recent changes to mail volume (i.e., decreases in first-class mail volume and increases in package volume).[97] Below is a selected list of the proposals contained in the USPS *Business Plan*:

- continued consolidation of mail processing facilities (known as the Network Rationalization Initiative);
- full implementation of revised postal service delivery standards;
- adjustments to staffing and the means of providing products and services at retail locations, including increases in "self-service" kiosks and reduced hours at selected retail locations;
- a shift to centralized and curbside mail delivery for both business and residential customers, where appropriate;
- an expanded scope of products and services offered at retail locations; and

- a move to five-day delivery of mail while maintaining six-day delivery of packages.[98]

Of the initiatives in the bulleted list above, the first two items are currently being implemented by the Postal Service. The third and fourth items have been implemented in part. The USPS arguably does not have authority to implement the final two items, and would likely require legislative action from Congress. Additional information on select initiatives developed and implemented (in full or in part) by the Postal Service is provided in the sections below.

Postal Service Delivery Standards[99]

The USPS's delivery standards are performance goals that reflect "the number of days after acceptance of a mail piece by which the sender and recipient can expect it to be delivered."[100] Delivery standards differ for each mail class and product. Since 2012, the Postal Service has phased-in revisions to its delivery standards for market dominant products.[101]

For example, as shown in **Table 5**, the length of delivery time for First-Class mail ranges from one to three days, while periodicals take between three and nine days.[102] Prior to the most recent revisions, the range for periodicals was from two to nine days and First-Class mail sent within a certain geographical boundary was generally guaranteed to be delivered overnight.[103]

Table 5. USPS Delivery Standard Ranges

Mail Class	End-to-End Range (days)
First-Class Mail	1-3
Periodicals	3-9
Standard Mail	3-10
Package Services	2-8

Source: 39 C.F.R. §121, Appendix A.

Notes: More detailed information on service delivery standards for specific regions is provided by the U.S. Postal Service Standards Map, which is a ZIP code-searchable map showing service delivery standard ranges (in number of days) for each mail class by both originating and destination ZIP codes. USPS's interactive service standards map is available at https://ribbs.usps.gov/ modernservicestandards/ ssmaps/find_map.cfm.

Table 6. USPS FY2015 Service Performance Targets and Percent On-Time

	Overnight		2-Day		3+ Days	
	Target % On-Time	**Actual % On-Time**	**Target % On-Time**	**Actual % On-Time**	**Target % On-Time**	**Actual % On-Time**
First-Class Mail						
Single-piece letters	96.8	*95.8*	96.5	*94.0*	95.3	***77.3***
Presort letters/postcards	96.8	*96.0*	96.5	*93.8*	95.3	***88.0***
Flats	96.8	***83.2***	96.5	***79.8***	95.3	***65.3***
Parcels	96.8	***84.8***	96.5	***84.2***	95.3	*73.7*
Periodicals						
In-county	-	-	-	-	91.0	*77.7*
Outside-county	-	-	-	-	91.0	***77.6***
Standard Mail *Saturation letters*	-	-	-	-	91.0	91.5
Saturation flats/parcels	-	-	-	-	91.0	*87.0*
Carrier route mail	-	-	-	-	91.0	*82.0*
Every Door Direct MailTM	-	-	-	-	91.0	***78.5***
Letters	-	-	-	-	91.0	*85.8*
Flats	-	-	-	-	91.0	***73.8***
Parcels	-	-	-	-	91.0	98.1
Package Services						
Parcel post/Alaska bypass -	-	-	-	90.0	NA	
Bound printed–flats	-	-	-	-	90.0	***45.2***
Bound printed–parcels	-	-	-	-	90.0	99.4
Media matter/library mail	-	-	-	-	90.0	91.2

Source: U.S. Postal Regulatory Commission, *Annual Compliance Determination Report FY2015*, March 28, 2016, pp. 132-143, at http://www.prc.gov/sites/default/files/reports/Final_2015_ACD.pdf.

Notes: *Periodicals*, *Standard Mail*, and *Package Services* do not have overnight or 2-day targets. Table excludes First-Class international mail, which had combined target of 94% and on-time % ranging from 75.6% to 96.1%. *Flats* are rectangular mailpieces that exceed the dimensions of letter-size mail, but may still be processed as mail rather than parcels or packages. *Saturation (and High Density) Letters, Flats, and Parcels* are mailpieces sent at reduced prices due to the total volume of pieces sent by the mailer. *Carrier Route* is category (and price) of mail presorted and prepared by the mailer. *Every Door Direct MailTM* uses "postal customer" in place of a delivery address for mailing of advertising mail. *Alaska Bypass* allows mailers to ship palletized goods to and from certain points within rural Alaska at parcel post rates.

The delivery standards are not, however, a guarantee of specific delivery times. Based on the delivery standards, the Postal Service sets "Service Performance Targets," which are the percentage of time it expects to meet its delivery standards. **Table 6** shows FY2015 service performance targets and the USPS's actual percent on-time score for each category of market dominant mail. Actual percent on-time scores that fail to meet the percent on-time service performance targets are shown in italics. Those that are more than 10 percentage points below the percent on-time performance targets are in italics and bold.

In FY2015, USPS failed to meet its percent on-time performance targets for nearly all types of market dominant mail, including all categories of First-Class mail. Single-piece letters and flats that fell within the 3-day processing window met USPS's on-time performance standards about 77% and 65% of the time, respectively. In many other instances, on-time performance was more than 10% below the USPS's targets. According to the PRC's *Annual Compliance Report*, the USPS largely attributes these results to (1) winter weather storms, (2) insufficient air transportation capacity, and (3) staff realignments and other issues related to the network rationalization initiative, which is discussed below.[104]

Restructuring the Processing and Delivery Network[105]

The revised delivery standards discussed above are part of the USPS's broader Network Rationalization Initiative (NRI).[106] The NRI involves the changes to delivery standards (discussed above) and the closure and consolidation of selected mail processing facilities. The USPS argues these changes are necessary to (1) address recent changes to mail volume (i.e., decreases in first-class mail volume and increases in package volume) and (2) improve the efficiency of the overall postal delivery network.[107]

The NRI was implemented in two phases. Phase I is complete and Phase II has been partially implemented beginning in January 2015. In late 2015, the Postal Service decided to defer until 2016 most of the remaining mail processing plant consolidations that were scheduled as part of Phase II.[108] Further, in February 2016, the Postal Service acknowledged that the Phase II closures failed to capture the savings originally projected.[109] In its filing to the PRC, the USPS reported $64.3 million in savings and $130.2 million in costs attributable to Phase II of the NRI, which is a net loss of $65.9

million.[110] The filing, however, did not state if the costs were a factor in USPS's decision to halt the closures.[111]

In comparison, the USPS reported an annualized savings of $865 million from Phase I. The USPS states that the increased costs of Phase II are due to "unplanned package growth and workload shift."[112] The U.S. Postal Service OIG, however, argues that the consolidations have likely led to increased transportation costs and it encourages greater transparency regarding USPS transportation contracts.[113]

Unanticipated Effects of the NRI on the USPS Workforce

A 2015 USPS OIG report found that the NRI had some unanticipated effects on USPS operations, including the USPS workforce.[114] The report asserted that revised service standards under the NRI allowed the USPS to expedite mail processing timelines, which prompted the agency to transition 5,000 employees from night to day shifts.[115] The shift changes have resulted in decreased differential pay and additional training for new jobs for some employees, according to the report.[116] The report further asserted that shift changes required larger mail processing plants to re-bid hundreds of jobs to employees with the new shift times, noting that the job bidding process can take "several months to complete."[117]

Restructuring the Retail Business

Two reforms the USPS included in its *Five-Year Business Plan* were (1) a proposal to move from six- to five-day delivery of all or most classes of mail, but maintain or expand package delivery, and (2) a proposal to further reduce retail post office hours to better align them with estimates of operational demand.

Six- to Five-Day Delivery[118]

One reform that the USPS has repeatedly proposed in recent years is to move from six- to five-day delivery of all or most classes of mail—typically, USPS's market dominant products, such as first-class mail, standard mail (i.e., advertising mail), and periodicals.[119] To maximize revenue from the competitive portion of its product line, however, USPS proposes maintaining six-day delivery of packages, or further expanding its Sunday package delivery services.[120]

Opponents of reducing USPS's delivery days argue that it will have a negative effect on postal delivery standards, which—according to the PRC's FY2015 *Annual Compliance Report*—have already suffered following the closure and consolidation of postal processing facilities prior to the 2015 suspension of the process.[121]

According to economic estimates prepared for the PRC, shifting to five-day delivery of mail while maintaining Saturday delivery of packages would increase revenues by an estimated $912 million to $1.677 billion.[122] The estimated net profit would be less, however, due to two factors. The Postal Service may incur additional labor costs due to increased mail volume on Mondays.[123]

Also, proposals may differ regarding Saturday operating hours at local post offices. If local post offices are open, there would be additional operational costs. In contrast, some customers may mail fewer items or choose another service for shipping packages if their local post office is closed on Saturday, potentially leading to lost revenue in competitive products. The PRC report based its estimation on a model where post offices remained open but did not sort or dispatch letter mail.[124] Under this scenario, the PRC report estimated that the annual net savings to the Postal Service would be between $625 million and $1.393 billion.[125]

Retail Post Office Closures[126]

In 2012, the USPS announced a plan to reduce hours at 13,000 "low foot traffic" U.S. Post Offices in rural communities. The Post Office Structure Plan, commonly referred to as the "POStPlan," is, according to the USPS, an initiative intended to prevent closures of postal retail facilities by reducing operational hours at selected locations. According to communications from the PRC, most POStPlan facilities are small and often in rural areas, though neither term (i.e., "small" or "rural") has been defined by either the USPS or the PRC for the purpose of identifying specific retail postal facilities.[127]

Table 7 below provides data on the number of USPS retail facilities in existence at the end of each fiscal year from FY2010 through FY2015.[128]

Impact of Postal Facility Closures on Postal Workforce

The USPS has implemented several non-personnel initiatives that have reportedly affected the size and cost of its workforce. GAO and the PRC, for example, reported that streamlining and consolidating activities associated with the POStPlan and NRI have reduced the number of career employees and work hours for postmasters, clerks, mailhandlers, and equipment maintenance personnel.[129] According to a 2014 GAO report, the USPS projects the POStPlan will generate $347.2 million in savings through FY2016.[130] The GAO report also discusses other initiatives to streamline and consolidate operations that have affected workforce size and cost, such as changes to delivery schedules and modes.[131]

Table 7. Total USPS Retail Postal Facilities, FY2010-FY2015

	2010	2011	2012	2013	2014	2015
Post Offices	27,077	26,927	26,755	26,670	26,669	26,615
Classified stations, branches, and carrier annexes	5,451	5,219	5,102	5,032	4,993	4,991
Total USPS-managed	**32,528**	**32,146**	**31,857**	**31,702**	**31,662**	**31,606**
Contract Postal Units	2,931	2,904	2,792	2,718	2,660	2,504
Village Post Offices	0	0	47	385	759	874
Community Post Offices	763	706	673	629	560	536
Total Contractor-operated	3,694	3,610	3,512	3,732	3,979	3,914
Total offices, stations, and branches (USPS-managed and contractor-operated)	**36,222**	**35,756**	**35,369**	**35,434**	**35,641**	**35,520**

Source: U.S. Postal Service *Annual Report to Congress, FY2013*, at http://about.usps.com/publications/annualreport-comprehensive-statement-2013/annualreport2013_001.htm; and U.S. Postal Regulatory Commission, *Annual Compliance Determination Report FY2015*, March 28, 2016, p. 148.

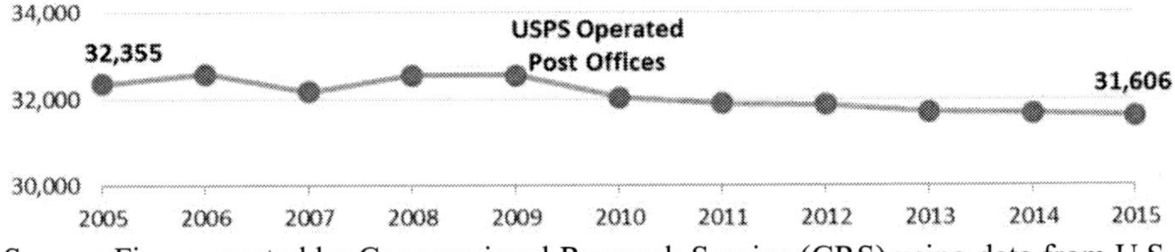

Source: Figure created by Congressional Research Service (CRS) using data from U.S. Postal Service "Decade of Facts and Figures," at http://about.usps.com/who-we-are/postal-facts/decade-of-facts-and-figures.htm.

Notes: "Total retail post offices" includes contractor-owned-and-operated postal facilities.

Figure 8. USPS Retail Postal Facilities; FY2005-FY2015.

Possible Issues Facing the USPS Workforce[132]

Achievement of Workforce Reduction Goals

The USPS anticipates its strategic initiatives, which appear to include the aforementioned workforce initiatives, would reduce its career workforce to around 404,000 employees by FY2017.[133] The number of career employees, however, has not decreased at projected annual rates. While USPS anticipated the career workforce to decrease by about 84,000 employees from FY2012 to FY2014, it decreased by 40,158 employees over the two-year time period.[134] Consequently, achievement of workforce reduction targets for FY2015-FY2017 might become more difficult. It is unclear if USPS still intends to reach its FY2017 workforce reduction goal, as the agency has not explicitly revised it since April 2013. Additional separation incentives, or other workforce reduction initiatives, might be needed, however, if the USPS intends to achieve the goal.

The USPS's ability to achieve its workforce reduction goal might be affected by unanticipated policy changes or actions of stakeholders. According to a 2014 GAO report, for example, the USPS's FY2017 workforce reduction goal assumed the adoption of actions that would impact workforce size that have not occurred, such as adoption of six-day package/five-day mail delivery service.[135] In addition, USPS postponed implementation of Phase II of the NRI, which was projected to affect around 15,000 employees.[136] Finally, postal labor unions have made efforts to curtail reductions to the career workforce. For example, in September 2014, the American Postal Workers Union (APWU) won an arbitration award that was projected to create 9,000 positions within the clerk craft function, at least 3,000 of which must be career positions.[137]

Limitations on Use of Non-Career Employees

The USPS's use of certain non-career employees is governed by postal labor union contracts, which limit the total number of non-career employees that can comprise the USPS workforce. Union contracts current through 2015 and 2016 raised the number of non-career employees that can be used for certain functions. The 2006-2011 National Association of Letter Carriers (NALC) contract raised the limit on the total number of covered non-career employees to 15% of the total number of career carriers in a district,[138] compared to 3.5% in the 2006-2011 contract.[139] (**Table 8**).[140]

Table 8. Contract Limitations on the Number of Selected Non-Career Employees

Labor Union	Affected Non-Career Employee Positions	Past Contract Limit	Current Contract Limit
American Postal Workers Union (APWU)	Casuals (past limit) Postal Service Employees (current limit)	6% of the total number of career employees covered by the contract per districta	20% of career employees in the clerk craft per districtb
National Postal Mail Handlers Union (NPHMU)	Casuals (past limit) Mail Handler Assistants (current limit)	12.5% of the total number of employees covered by the contract per installation	15% of career mail handlers per district 20% of career mail handlers per installation 5% of the total number of career employees covered by the contract per installation (casuals)
National Association of Letter Carriers (NALC)	Transitional employees (past limit) CityCarrier Assistants (current limit)	3.5% of the total number of city carriers covered by the contract 6% of the total number ofcareer city letter carriers per districtc	15% of career city letter carriers per districtd

Source: CRS analysis of contracts between the USPS and the American Postal Workers Union, National Postal Mail Handlers Union, and National Association of Letter Carriers; information provided by the Postal Regulatory Commission on August 14, 2015, and August 26, 2015.

Notes: Limitations listed under "current limit" are stipulated by postal union contracts current through 2015 and 2016. Limitations listed under "past limit" were stipulated by postal union contracts that expired in 2010 or 2011. A postal "district" refers to a ZIP code area, and a postal "installation" refers to a post office. In contracts that expired in 2010 or 2011, non-career employees were referred to as "casuals" or "transitional employees." These positions have been largely replaced by Postal Service Employees (PSEs), City Carrier Assistants (CCAs), and Mail Handler Assistants (MHAs), though some casuals still exist.

[a] Within the 6% limitation, non-career casuals could not exceed 11% of career clerk craft employees at installations with 200 or more *workyears* of employment in the regular workforce. A *workyear* is equivalent to 2,080 hours of work. For more information, see CRS, *Federal Workforce Statistics Sources: OPM and OMB*; and Circular A-11, pp. 273-274, at https://www.whitehouse.gov/sites/default/ files/omb/assets/ a11_current_year/a11_2015.pdf.

[b] The 2010-2015 APWU contract placed additional limits on retail (window) clerks. In larger offices (Level 22 and above), PSEs working retail windows could not exceed 10% of the career retail clerks in the installation. In smaller offices (Level 21 and below), PSEs could not exceed 20% of the career retail clerks.

[c] In addition, the 2006-2011 NALC contract required installations with 200 or more *workyears* of employment in the regular workforce to be 88% staffed by career letter carriers.

[d] The 2011-2016 NALC contract allows USPS to exceed the 15% limitation and hire an additional 8,000 CCAs to provide new products and services. The number of additional CCAs cannot exceed 8% of the total number of career city delivery carriers in the district for any one reporting period.

The USPS's ability to maintain or increase its use of certain non-career employees will depend on contract negotiations. Some labor unions seem to oppose increased use of non-career employees, which appear to have affected negotiations for certain unions. For example, negotiations between the USPS and the APWU ended without an agreement on May 28, 2015. [141] The APWU subsequently issued a press release stating that "proposed changes to the [USPS] workforce structure were completely unacceptable."[142] The press release then cited USPS workforce proposals for the new contract, which included, among other things, an increase in the percentage of non-career employees. The APWU workforce proposals, in contrast, called for more career employees.[143] On July 8, 2016, an arbitration panel issued a new APWU contract that maintained current levels of covered non-career employees.[144]

Lower caps on the percentage of non-career employees might have implications for the size and cost of the USPS's workforce. According to a 2014 GAO report, the USPS asserted that it is close to reaching current caps on non-career employees.[145] Lower caps, therefore, might require the USPS to reduce the number of non-career employees, which might prompt changes to the agency's workforce composition in ways that might increase personnel costs. For instance, compensation costs might increase if the USPS increases the number of career employees to comply with lower caps, either through additional hires or transitioning non-career employees to career positions. Alternatively, overtime pay cost might increase if the USPS reduces the number of non-career employees that were being used in place of career employees earning overtime.

Employee Morale

Some postal labor unions and Members of Congress have expressed concern about employee morale at the USPS, particularly amid the agency's efforts to reduce the size and cost of its workforce. For example, the APWU asserted that post office closures and mail processing plant consolidations are lowering employee morale.[146] On March 5, 2014, Senator Heidi Heitkamp sent a letter to the Postmaster General that highlighted challenges identified by USPS employees in North Dakota that might lead to low morale, including long hours, poor working conditions, a lack of training, and a lack of managerial focus on addressing such issues.[147]

On July 9, 2015, Senator Heitkamp introduced the Rural Postal Act of 2015.[148] The bill seeks to, among other things, improve employee morale at the USPS by establishing a Chief Morale Officer.[149] The Officer would be responsible for developing national initiatives[150] that address employee morale and factors that might influence morale, such as factors related to working conditions, communication, and training. For example, the bill would require national initiatives to address wages and the balance between temporary and career employees. The bill also proposes the establishment of Regional Morale Officers, who would be responsible for (1) implementing the national initiatives; (2) holding monthly roundtables with employees to discuss concerns related to working conditions, staffing, communication, and training; (3) submitting biennial feedback reports to the Chief Morale Officer; and (4) communicating regularly with other Regional Morale Officers and the Chief Morale Officer to provide progress updates on achieving the initiatives.[151] As of August 10, 2016, there has been no committee or floor action on this bill.[152]

Further Postal Reform Issues for Congress

Updating the Postal Fleet[153]

To fulfill its mission of providing "prompt, reliable, and efficient"[154] postal services to its customers, the USPS has a fleet of approximately 190,000 delivery vehicles.[155] These vehicles transport more than 153 billion pieces of mail each year[156] to more than 150 million delivery points.[157] Approximately 75% of the delivery fleet (142,000 vehicles) is comprised of long-life vehicles

(LLVs),[158] which have an expected useful life of 24 years.[159] Many LLVs were purchased in the late 1980s and early 1990s, and have now met or exceeded their life expectancy.[160] Indeed, the average age of an LLV reached 23 years in 2015.[161] Moreover, the USPS OIG determined the current fleet can only meet delivery needs through FY2017.[162]

Given the need to replace much of its aging delivery fleet, the USPS has proposed acquiring up to180,000 new delivery vehicles through its Next Generation Delivery Vehicle (NGDV) acquisition program.[163] The NGDVs would cost between $25,000 and $35,000 each, and have a life span of 20 years.[164] The new fleet would differ from the current LLV fleet in several ways, notably that they would be configured to handle a larger number of packages[165]—which analysts believe will continue to grow in volume in coming years.[166] The NGDVs would also use less fuel and more advanced safety features than the current LLV fleet.[167]

The NGDV acquisition program will take an estimated five to seven years to complete.[168] In January, 2015, the USPS issued a Request for Information (RFI), which provided prospective suppliers with the specifications of the NGDVs, and invited interested parties to submit information that demonstrated their ability to meet the manufacturing and production requirements of the program. Based on responses to the RFI, the USPS developed a list of "prequalified" suppliers who showed they could meet the program's requirements.[169] Only the prequalified suppliers are eligible to participate in the next phase of the program.[170]

In October, 2015, the USPS issued a Request for Proposal (RFP) seeking a qualified supplier to design and manufacture six "fully functional" prototypes of its NGDVs.[171] The USPS anticipates that this phase of the program—the design, build, and testing of the prototypes—will take about two years to complete.[172]

The final phase of the program, the production and delivery of the NGDV fleet, would begin in 2017.[173] At that point, a second RFP would be released, which would establish the final NGDV production requirements, and indicate whether the USPS will purchase the vehicles, lease them, or both. The USPS has stated that while it is likely that just one sup$_{17}$lier would be awarded the contract, it is possible that more than one supplier may be selected.[4]

Nonpostal Products and Servicesim

The PAEA defines *postal services* as "the delivery of letters, printed matter, or mailable packages, including acceptance, collection, sorting, transportation, or other functions ancillary thereto" and prohibits the USPS from offering all but a limited number of excepted nonpostal products and services.[176] This restriction prevents the Postal Service from offering or developing new nonpostal products (e.g., expanded banking and financial services) or expanding into new markets that might increase its market share and revenue.[177]

Under the PAEA, the Postal Service is currently authorized to offer 11 nonpostal products and services, including two market dominant and nine competitive products.[178] The two market dominant products are

- USPS/public sector alliances, e.g., MoverSource, which allows the USPS to provide free change-of-address services by including moving tips and related advertisements;[179] and
- philatelic sales intended for stamp collectors, e.g., uncut press sheets, framed stamps, binders for storing stamps, and philatelic guides.[180]

The nine competitive products are

- private sector advertising on USPS.com, within U.S. post offices, or in other postal venues;[181]
- licensing of USPS's copyrights and trademarks;[182]
- mail service promotions, which "allow merchants who offer web-based customers the ability to create mail pieces through an online service." Prices for these products are negotiated between the merchant and the Postal Service;[183]
- sale of officially licensed USPS retail products;[184]
- U.S. Passport photo services;[185]
- photocopying services; [186]
- rental, leasing, and non-sale of USPS property;[187]
- use of USPS training facility and courses;[1] and
- the USPS Electronic Postmark (EPM) program, which "authorizes vendors to provide their customers with Postal Service-authorized timestamps."[189]

In FY2015, revenues from nonpostal market dominant products were $75 million and expenses were $13 million, for a net gain of $62 million.[190] For nonpostal competitive products, revenues were $106 million and expenses were $17 million, for a net gain of $89 million.[191] This was an increase of 13% and 4% from FY2014 nonpostal market dominant and competitive revenues, respectively.[192]

The Postal Service is also authorized, with limitations, to conduct short-term market tests that may include nonpostal products.[193] Market-tests are generally limited to two years and have included the sale of gift cards, a same-day delivery service (Metro PostTM), and an international eCommerce shipping service (GeM Merchant).[194] The USPS OIG suggested grocery delivery as another possible market test in its June 2016 OIG Blog post.[195]

Select postal reform legislation introduced in the 113th and 114th Congresses would provide the USPS with authority to offer additional nonpostal products and services. The nonpostal products and services covered in recent bills include

- public internet access;[196]
- drivers' license services;[197]
- hunting and fishing license services; 198
- voter registration; [199] and
- postal banking and financial services.[200]

Further, legislation introduced in the 114th Congress, such as S. 2051, *Improving Postal Operations, Service, and Transparency Act of 2015* (iPOST Act) and H.R. 5714, *Postal Service Reform Act of 2016*, includes provisions that would allow the USPS to offer a range of nonpostal products and services that are currently prohibited under the PAEA.[201]

Postal Banking[202]

In looking for ways to grow USPS's nonpostal products and services, one option is to expand the financial services it offers (e.g., international money orders, prepaid cards). The USPS offered select financial products in the 20th century, but they have not been available since the termination of the Postal Savings System in 1967.[203]

One reason that postal financial services are still raised as a potentially beneficial product line may be the example provided by other nations. Countries with some form of postal financial services include the United Kingdom, France, Japan, Germany, South Korea, and Brazil, in addition to many others.[204] These examples also highlight the numerous different models that a postal system can utilize to provide financial services. In some cases, the postal service offers its own financial products through a separate entity established within the postal department. In other cases, the postal service facilitates the sale of financial services that are managed by a private financial institution. Some nations have implemented a hybrid of these two approaches. For example, South Korea uses a system wherein its postal service (Korea Post) offers its own financial services while also handling deposits made to private banks.[205]

To further explore this idea, the USPS OIG issued a white paper in early 2014 to study whether the USPS is well-positioned to offer financial services.[206] In this report, the USPS OIG determined that financial services are the best opportunities for the USPS to generate new revenue. In addition, the report estimated there would be significant demand for these services from populations currently underserved by private banks.

Following the publication of the initial white paper, the USPS OIG completed a second study in 2015 that examined the statutory authority required to offer financial services and offered possible models that could be used.[207] First, the report stated that the USPS could simply expand its current offering of financial products, which includes paper money orders, gift cards, and check cashing. This approach would provide limited growth opportunities, but would also incur relatively low implementation costs and is permissible under current statutory authority. The USPS OIG estimates that after a five-year period of developing these services, the USPS could generate $1.1 billion in additional revenue annually.[208]

Beyond this approach, the white paper also identified four alternative models that draw heavily on the experience of other countries. For each of these approaches, the upfront costs would be higher and the USPS OIG states additional statutory authority would be needed.[209] These four approaches are (1) a partnership with one outside firm to offer services through the USPS; (2) partnerships with multiple outside firms that are specialized for each individual product; (3) a marketplace model wherein the USPS facilitates many options for each financial service; and (4) a full-fledged postal bank, which would offer financial products wholly managed by the USPS or an entity within the agency.[210]

Arguments For and against Postal Banking

The work of the USPS OIG began a national conversation around the merits of developing postal financial services at the USPS, with many advocates for and against the concept. As mentioned above, proponents of postal financial services believe that such an expansion would offer financial services to underserved populations and provide needed revenue to the postal service at a time when demand for their traditional product line of first class mail delivery is declining.

Recently, many journalists and organizations have recommended a postal savings system as a way to reach households and individuals that do not currently make use of an insured financial institution and instead rely on alternative financial services (AFS). According to a 2013 report from the Federal Deposit Insurance Corporation (FDIC), this population is relatively large. [211] The report found that 7.7% of all U.S. households were unbanked, meaning they had no account at an insured financial institution, while 20% of households were considered underbanked, meaning they had used AFS in the previous 12 months.[212]

On the other side of the debate over postal financial services are those who believe the expanded services would not generate revenue or would unfairly encroach on the private market for financial services. Specifically, some have critiqued the revenue forecasts developed by the USPS OIG and the assumption that the underserved populations trust the USPS more than other institutions.[213] Some have questioned whether there is a conflict between the two primary benefits that are currently suggested by postal banking advocates. Writing in the *Washington Post*, Charles Lane stated,

> At bottom, though, the problem with postal banking is a certain inherent tension between its policy objectives: is the primary purpose to help low-income people, or is it to help the postal service make more money to offset the irreversible decline of its bread-and-butter business, first-class mail?[214]

Without a more detailed estimate of the costs at which the USPS could profitably provide these services, the validity of this particular critique cannot be determined.

The U.S. Postal Savings System: 1911-1967

In evaluating the merits of expanding USPS financial products and services, many have looked to the USPS's own experience with postal banking in the first half of the 20th century. From 1911 until 1967, the USPS operated the U.S. Postal Savings System (PSS) throughout the United States. At its peak in the late 1940s, this system had more than 4 million depositors and $3.4 billion in accounts. The purpose of this system at the time of its creation was to "get money out of hiding, to attract savings of a large number of immigrants who were accustomed to savings at post offices in their native countries, and to provide safe depositories for people who had lost confidence in private banks."[215] This emphasis on reaching new underserved populations, providing an alternative beyond private institutions, and looking to international examples mirrors many of the arguments being made on behalf of postal financial services today.

Select Postal Banking Legislation

In the 113th Congress, Representative Cummings introduced H.R. 2690, *Innovate to Deliver Act of 2013*, which if enacted, would have expanded USPS's authority to offer nonpostal products and services, including "check-cashing services."[216]

As discussed in the 2015 USPS OIG report, a more comprehensive approach is for the Postal Service to become a chartered and licensed bank.[217] As a bank, the USPS would have authority to provide a range of financial services, such as savings accounts, personal loans, check cashing services, and insurance products.[218] In the 114th Congress, Representative Richmond introduced H.R. 4422 which, if enacted, would provide the Postal Service with authority to "provide basic financial services" including small-dollar loans, checking and savings accounts, and other services in the public interest.[219] Under the bill, the USPS would have authority to provide some of these services "alone, or in partnership with depository institutions."[220] The bill, however, stopped short of establishing a new postal banking system with a chartered and licensed USPS bank.

While the specific proposals in the USPS OIG white paper, in articles, and in legislation differ in the financial products they cover, each of the proposals appears to share certain characteristics and goals. Each leverages the nationwide service network and accessibility of the USPS. Further, each seeks to achieve one or both of two goals: reach populations that are underserved by current financial institutions or provide additional revenue opportunities to the USPS.

Appendix A. USPS Revenue and Volume by Mail Category and Class

Table A-1. USPS Revenue and Volume, by Mail Category and Class

Mail Category and Class	Revenue (thousands $)				Volume (thousands of pieces)			
	FY2014	FY2015	Change	Chg (%)	FY2014	FY2015	Change	Chg (%)
Market Dominant Mail								
First-Class	29,636,930	29,596,896	-40,034	-0.14%	64,683,808	63,305,152	-1,378,656	-2.13%
Mail								
Standard Mail	17,494,470	17,711,219	216,749	1.24%	80,374,260	80,090,273	-283,987	-0.35%
Periodicals	1,625,326	1,589,221	-36,105	-2.22%	6,044,715	5,838,175	-206,540	-3.42%
Mail								
Package	831,075	806,077	-24,998	-3.01%	548,470	564,576	16,106	2.94%
Services Mail								
U.S. Postal	-	-	-	-	438,643	354,628	-84,015	-19.15%
Service Mail								
Free Mail	-	-	-	-	45,989	45,135	-854	-1.86%
Ancillary and	2,016,591	1,924,730	-91,861	-4.56%	-	-	-	-
Special								
Services								
Other	1,162,137	798,198	-363,938	-31.30%	-	-	-	-
Market								
Dominant								
Revenue								
Total Market	52,766,529	52,426,341	-340,188	-0.64%	152,135,885	150,197,939	-1,937,946	-1.27%
Dominant								

Mail Category and Class	Revenue (thousands $)				Volume (thousands of pieces)			
	FY2014	FY2015	Change	Chg (%)	FY2014	FY2015	Change	Chg (%)
Competitive Mail								
Priority Mail	759,843	779,067	19,224	2.50%	36,231	35,705	-526	-1.45%
Express								
First-Class	1,417,618	1,689,112	271,494	19.20%	616,280	708,423	92,143	14.95%
Package								
Service								
Standard	503,804	474,340	-29,464	-5.80%	36,306	32,516	-3,790	-10.44%
Post								
Priority Mail	6,729,485	7,276,239	546,754	8.10%	897,900	992,190	94,290	10.50%
Parcel Select	2,528,944	3,298,476	769,533	30.40%	1,482,669	1,876,634	393,965	26.57%
Mail								
Parcel	138,619	152,301	13,682	9.90%	55,650	59,610	3,960	7.12%
Return								
Service Mail								
International	2,211,359	1,970,464	-240,895	10.90%	277,753	253,963	-23,790	-8.57%
Mail								
Ancillary and	710,019	785,790	75,771	10.70%	-	-	-	-
Special								
Services								
Other	88,100	99,049	10,949	12.40%	-	-	-	-
Competitive								
Revenue								
Total	15,087,791	16,524,838	1,437,047	9.52%	3,402,789	3,959,041	556,252	16.35%

Table A-1. (Continued)

Mail Category and Class	Revenue (thousands $)				Volume (thousands of pieces)			
	FY2014	FY2015	Change	Chg (%)	FY2014	FY2015	Change	Chg (%)
Competitive								
Total All Mail and Services	67,854,320	68,951,179	1,096,859	1.62%	155,538,674	154,156,980	-1,381,694	-0.89%

Source: U.S. Postal Service, Final Revenue, Pieces, and Weight by Classes of Mail and Special Services for Fiscal Year 2015, October 2015, at http://about.usps.com/who-we-are/financials/revenue-pieces-weight-reports/fy2015- q4.csv.

Notes: U.S. Postal Service Mail and Free Mail refer to mail services that the USPS provides at no charge, either for its own purposes or because they are statutorily required to provide the service at no charge (e.g., free mail for the blind). For descriptions of the specific products that fall within each service category and mail class, see U.S. Postal Regulatory Commission, Mail Classification Schedule, January 15, 2016, at http://www.prc.gov/mailclassification-schedule; and U.S. Postal Service, Glossary of Postal Terms, Publication 32, July 2013, at http://about.usps.com/publications/pub32.pdf.

APPENDIX B. POSTAL REFORM LEGISLATION INTRODUCED IN THE 113TH AND 114TH CONGRESSES

Table B-1. Selected Postal-Related Legislation Introduced in the 113th and 114th Congresses

Bill Number	Title	Sponsor	Committees	Selected Issue Area(s) Covered	Last Major Action
H.R. 5714(114th)	Postal Service Reform Act of 2016	Rep. Chaffetz, Jason (R-UT-3)	House Oversight and Government Reform; House Energy and Commerce; House Ways and Means	Multiple, including new postal service health program requiring eligible retiree enrollment in Medicare Parts A and B, USPS pension funding reform, 2.15% rate increase for market dominant products, authorization for nonpostal products, phased/voluntary conversion to centralized delivery.	Latest Major Action: 7/12/2016House Committee Consideration and Mark-up Session Held. Ordered to be Reported by Voice Vote.
H.R. 4656(114th)	Stop Postal Closures Act of 2016	Rep. Huffman, Jared (D-CA-2)	House Oversight and Government Reform	Moratorium on processing facility closures and consolidations, and reinstatement of July 2012 service delivery standards.	Latest Major Action: 3/1/2016 Referred to the House Committee on Oversight and Government Reform.

Table B-1. (Continued)

Bill Number	Title	Sponsor	Committees	Selected Issue Area(s) Covered	Last Major Action
H.R. 4422(114th)	POSTAL Act of 2015	Rep. Richmond, Cedric L. (D-LA-2)	House Oversight and Government Reform	Expanding scope of nonpostal products and services, specifically, basic financial services.	Latest Major Action: 2/1/2016 Referred to the House Committee on Oversight and Government Reform.
S. 2051(114th)	Improving Postal Operations, Service, and Transparency Act of 2015 (or iPost Act)	Sen. Carper, Thomas R. (D-DE)	Senate Homeland Security and Governmental Affairs	Multiple, including new postal service health program requiring eligible employee and retiree enrollment in Medicare Parts A, B and D, pension funding reform, reinstitutes exigent price increase for market dominant products, authorizes nonpostal products, keeps current service delivery standards, and authorizes shipment of wine, beer, and spirits.	Latest Major Action: 9/17/2015 Referred to Senate Homeland Security and Governmental Affairs Committee. Full Committee hearing held 1/21/2016, “Laying Out the Reality of the United States Postal Service.”
H.R. 3464(114th)	Defending Quality Postal Delivery for the Future Act	Rep. Grijalva, Raul M. (D-AZ-3)	House Oversight and Government Reform	Closure of USPS facilities.	Latest Major Action: 9/9/2015 Referred to the House Committee on Oversight and Government Reform.

Bill Number	Title	Sponsor	Committees	Selected Issue Area(s) Covered	Last Major Action
H.R. 3412(114th)	United States Postal Service Shipping Equity Act	Rep. Speier, Jackie (D-CA-14)	House Oversight and Government Reform; House Judiciary	Shipping of wine and malt beverages.	Latest Major Action: 7/29/2015 Referred to the House Committee on Oversight and Government Reform and HouseJudiciary Committee.
S. 1854(114th)	Postal Innovation Act	Sen. Booker, Cory A. (D-NJ)	Senate Homeland Security and Governmental Affairs	Multiple, including expanding scope of nonpostal products and services and shipment of beer, wine, and spirits.	Latest Major Action: 7/23/2015 Referred to Senate Homeland Security and Governmental Affairs Committee.
S. 1742(114th)	Rural Postal Act of 2015	Sen. Heitkamp, Heidi (D-ND)	Senate Homeland Security and Governmental Affairs	Multiple, including 6-day delivery, service delivery standards, and closure of USPS facilities.	Latest Major Action: 7/9/2015 Referred to Senate Homeland Security and Governmental Affairs Committee.
H.R. 1963(114th)	Federal Leadership in Energy Efficient Transportation Act of 2015	Rep. Huffman,Jared (D-CA-2)	House Oversight and Government Reform; House Energy and Commerce	Upgrades to postal fleet.	Latest Major Action: 4/24/2015 Referred to Subcommittee on Energy and Power.

Table B-1. (Continued)

Bill Number	Title	Sponsor	Committees	Selected Issue Area(s) Covered	Last Major Action
H.R. 1885(114th)	Securing Access to Rural Postal Services Act of 2015	Rep. Smith, Adrian (R-NE-3)	House Oversight and Government Reform	Closure of USPS facilities.	Latest Major Action: 4/16/2015Referred to the House Committee on Oversight and Government Reform.
H.R. 1837(114th)	Secure Delivery for America Act of 2015	Rep. Issa, Darrell E. (R-CA-49)	House Oversight and Government Reform	Centralized and curbside mail delivery.	Latest Major Action: 4/16/2015Referred to the House Committee on Oversight and Government Reform.
H.R. 1501(114th)	Moratorium on United States Postal Facilities Act	Rep.Lee, Barbara (D-CA-13)	House Oversight and Government Reform	Closure of USPS facilities.	Latest Major Action: 3/9/2015 Referred to the House Committee on Oversight and Government Reform.
H.R. 1198(114th)	Postal Employee Appeal Rights Amendments Act	Rep. Connolly, Gerald E. (D-VA-11)	House Oversight and Government Reform	USPS employee protection, e.g., right to appeal certain adverse actions to Merit Systems Protection Board.	Latest Major Action: 3/2/2015 Referred to the House Committee on Oversight and Government Reform.
S. 606(114th)	Postal Employee Appeal Rights Amendments Act of 2015	Sen. Tester, Jon (D-MT)	Senate Homeland Security and Governmental Affairs	USPS employee protection, e.g., right to appeal certain adverse actions to Merit Systems Protection Board.	Latest Major Action: 2/26/2015Referred to Senate Homeland Security and Governmental Affairs Committee.

Bill Number	Title	Sponsor	Committees	Selected Issue Area(s) Covered	Last Major Action
H.R. 784(114th)	Protect Overnight Delivery Act	Rep. DeLauro, Rosa L. (D-CT-3)	House Oversight and Government Reform	Service delivery standards.	Latest Major Action: 2/5/2015 Referred to the House Committee on Oversight and Government Reform.
H.R. 5377(113th)	Postal Facilities Preservation and Sales Reform Act	Rep. Serrano, Jose E. (D-NY-15)	House Oversight and Government Reform	Closure of USPS facilities.	Latest Major Action: 7/31/2014Referred to the House Committee on Oversight and Government Reform.
H.R. 5179(113th)	POSTAL Act of 2014	Rep. Richmond, Cedric L. (D-LA-2)	House Oversight and Government Reform	Expanding scope of nonpostal products and services, specifically, basic financial services.	Latest Major Action: 7/23/2014Referred to the House Committee on Oversight and Government Reform.
H.R. 4670(113th)	Secure Delivery for America Act of 2014	Rep. Issa, Darrell E. (R-CA-49)	House Oversight and Government Reform	Centralized and curbside mail delivery.	Latest Major Action: 5/21/2014 Ordered to be Reported (Amended) by the Yeas and Nays: 18 - 13.
H.R. 4174(113th)	Alaska Bypass Modernization Act of 2014	Rep. Issa, Darrell E. (R-CA-49)	House Oversight and Government Reform	Air carrier requirements and product rates in the stateof Alaska.	Latest Major Action: 3/12/2014 House Committee Consideration and Mark-up Session Held. Ordered to be Reported by Voice Vote.

Table B-1. (Continued)

Bill Number	Title	Sponsor	Committees	Selected Issue Area(s) Covered	Last Major Action
H.R. 4011(113th)	Alaska Bypass Fair Competition Act of 2014	Rep. Issa, Darrell E. (R-CA-49)	House Oversight and Government Reform	Air carrier requirements in the state of Alaska.	Latest Major Action: 2/11/2014 House Committee Consideration and Mark-up Session Held. Ordered to be Reported by Voice Vote.
H.R. 3963(113th)	Federal Leadership in Energy Efficient Transportation Act of 2014	Rep. Huffman, Jared (D-CA-2)	House Oversight and Government Reform; House Energy and Commerce	Upgrades to postal fleet.	Latest Major Action: 2/7/2014 Referred to Subcommittee on Energy and Power.
H.R. 3910(113th)	Expand Nonpostal Services to Americans Act	Rep. Cohen, Steve (D-TN-9)	House Oversight and Government Reform	Expanding the scope of nonpostal products and services offered.	Latest Major Action: 1/16/2014 Referred to the House Committee on Oversight and Government Reform.
H.R. 3801(113th)	To repeal the reductions in military retirement benefits made by the Bipartisan Budget Act of 2013 and to	Rep. Issa, Darrell E. (R-CA-49)	House Armed Services; House Oversight and Government Reform	Five-day delivery.	Latest Major Action: 12/19/2013Referred to the House Armed Services Committee and House Committee on Oversight and Government Reform.

Bill Number	Title	Sponsor	Committees	Selected Issue Area(s) Covered	Last Major Action
	authorize the United States Postal Service to implement a modified Saturday delivery schedule.				
S. 1486(113th)	Postal Reform Act of 2014	Sen. Carper, Thomas R. (D-DE)	Senate Homeland Security and Governmental Affairs	Multiple, including prefunding of RHBF, service delivery standards, and closure of USPS facilities.	Latest Major Action: 7/31/2014 Placed on Senate Legislative Calendar under General Orders. Calendar No. 523.
H.R. 2748(113th)	Postal Reform Act of 2013	Rep. Issa, Darrell E. (R-CA-49)	House Oversight and Government Reform; House Education and the Workforce	Multiple, including post office closures and five-day delivery.	Latest Major Action: 1/2/2015 Placed on the Union Calendar, Calendar No. 564.
H.R. 2690(113th)	Innovate to Deliver Act of 2013	Rep. Cummings, Elijah E. (D-MD-7)	House Oversight and Government Reform; House Judiciary	Multiple, including shipping of alcohol and expanding the scope of products and services offered at retail locations.	Latest Major Action: 9/13/2013 Referred to the Subcommittee on Crime, Terrorism, HomelandSecurity, and Investigations.

Table B-1. (Continued)

Bill Number	Title	Sponsor	Committees	Selected Issue Area(s) Covered	Last Major Action
H.R. 2615(113th)	Securing Access to Rural Postal Services Act of 2013	Rep. Smith, Adrian (R-NE-3)	House Oversight and Government Reform	Closure of USPS facilities in rural communities.	Latest Major Action: 7/8/2013 Referred to the House Committee on Oversight and Government Reform.
H.R. 2459(113th)	Protect Overnight Delivery Act	Rep. DeLauro, Rosa L. (D-CT-3)	House Oversight and Government Reform	Service delivery standards.	Latest Major Action: 6/20/2013 Referred to the House Committee on Oversight and Government Reform.
H.R. 1718(113th)	United States Postal Service Shipping Equity Act	Rep. Speier, Jackie (D-CA-14)	House Oversight and Government Reform; House Judiciary	Shipping of wine and malt beverages.	Latest Major Action: 6/14/2013 Referred to the Subcommittee on Crime, Terrorism, HomelandSecurity, and Investigations.
H.R. 1431(113th)	Postal Employee Appeal Rights Amendments Act of 2013	Rep. Connolly, Gerald E. (D-VA-11)	House Oversight and Government Reform	USPS employee protection, e.g., right to appeal certain adverse actions to Merit Systems Protection Board.	Latest Major Action: 4/9/2013 Referred to the House Committee on Oversight and Government Reform.

Bill Number	Title	Sponsor	Committees	Selected Issue Area(s) Covered	Last Major Action
S. 686(113th)	Postal Employee Appeal Rights Amendments Act of 2013	Sen. Pryor, Mark L. (D-AR)	Senate Homeland Security and Governmental Affairs	USPS employee protection, e.g., right to appeal certain adverse actions to Merit Systems Protection Board.	Latest Major Action: 2/13/2013 Referred to Senate Homeland Security and Governmental Affairs Committee.
H.R. 1016(113th)	Community Post Office Relocation Act	Rep. Peters, Scott H. (D-CA-52)	House Oversight and Government Reform	USPS real property.	Latest Major Action: 3/6/2013 Referred to the House Committee on Oversight and Government Reform.
H.R. 1006(113th)	Postal Executive Accountability Act	Rep. Griffith, H. Morgan (R-VA-9)	House Oversight and Government Reform	Pay, bonuses, and benefits for USPS officers and senior executive positions.	Latest Major Action: 3/6/2013 Referred to the House Committee on Oversight and Government Reform.
H.R. 961(113th)	United States Postal Service Stabilization Act of 2013	Rep. Lynch, Stephen F. (D-MA-8)	House Oversight and Government Reform	Calculation of USPS's contributions to the Federal Employees Retirement System (FERS) for its employees.	Latest Major Action: 3/5/2013 Referred to the House Committee on Oversight and Government Reform.
H.R. 630(113th)	Postal Service Protection Act of 2013	Rep. DeFazio, Peter A. (D-OR-4)	House Oversight and Government Reform; House Judiciary	Multiple, including prefunding of RHBF and closure of USPS facilities.	Latest Major Action:4/8/2013 Referred to the Subcommittee on Crime, Terrorism, HomelandSecurity, and Investigations.

Table B-1. (Continued)

Bill Number	Title	Sponsor	Committees	Selected Issue Area(s) Covered	Last Major Action
S. 316(113th)	Service Protection Act of 2013	Sen. Sanders, Bernard (I-VT)	Senate Homeland Security and Governmental Affairs	Multiple, including prefunding of RHBF and closure of USPS facilities.	Latest Major Action: 2/13/2013 Referred to Senate Homeland Security and Governmental Affairs Committee.

Source: CRS analysis using the Legislative Information System of the U.S. Congress (LIS), available at http://lis.gov/.

Notes: Results include all legislation listed under the drop-down menu topic titled "Postal Service (USPS)", with the following exceptions: post office naming bills, bills to establish commemorative or semi-postal stamps, bills to establish new postal ZIP codes. Postal-related provisions contained within omnibus budget and appropriations bills have also been excluded.

End Notes

[1] P.L. 91-375.

[2] Post Office Act of 1872 (17 Stat. 283).

[3] U.S. Postal Service, *The United States Postal Service: An American History 1775-2006*, November 2012, pp. 38-39, at http://about.usps.com/publications/pub100.pdf.

[4] Ibid.

[5] Change in total mail volume (in pieces) from 2006 to 2015 was 213.1 billion to 154.2 billion, or a drop of 58.9 billion pieces. U.S. Postal Service "Decade of Facts and Figures," at http://about.usps.com/who-we-are/postal-facts/decade-offacts-and-figures.htm.

[6] See "Impact of the Great Recession on the Postal Service," within U.S. Postal Regulatory Commission, *Rate Adjustment Due to Extraordinary or Exceptional Circumstances: Order Granting Exigent Price Increase*, Docket R2013-11, December 24, 2013, pp. 39-45, at http://www.prc.gov/docs/88/88645/Order_1926.pdf.

[7] U.S. Postal Service, *FY2016 Integrated Financial Plan*, November 20, 2015, p. 2, at http://about.usps.com/who-weare/financials/integrated-financial-plans/fy2016.pdf.

[8] This section authored by Michelle D. Christensen, Analyst in Government Organization and Management (7-0764).

[9] Under §102 of the Postal Accountability and Enhancement Act of 2006 (PAEA,), the USPS is prohibited from offering most nonpostal products and services. The PAEA allowed the USPS to continue offering 11 groups of "grandfathered" nonpostal products that had been offered prior to enactment of the PAEA. See section of this report titled "Nonpostal Products and Services" for additional information.

[10] Reference text is missed.

[11] U.S. Postal Service, *FY2015 Report on Form 10-K*, Washington, DC, 2015, p. 12, at http://about.usps.com/who-weare/financials/10k-reports/fy2015.pdf (hereafter, *FY2015 Report on Form 10-K).*

[12] Additionally, an advance appropriation of $41 million provided in the FY2015 FSGG Appropriations Act became available for obligation and expenditure at the start of FY2016. For this reason, the total payment to the Postal Service Fund for FY2016 is $96.075 million ($41 million + $55.075 million). See Division E of.

[13] Revenue Forgone Reform Act of 1993 (RFRA, Title VII). For additional information, see CRS Report RS21025, *The Postal Revenue Forgone Appropriation: Overview and Current Issues*, by Kevin R. Kosar. This author has left CRS. For questions about the Revenue Forgone Reform Act, please contact Michelle D. Christensen (7-0764).

[14] 39 U.S.C. §2003.

[15] Ibid.

[16] U.S. Postal Service, *FY2015 Report on Form 10-K*, pp. 31-32.

[17] 39 U.S.C. §2005(a). Currently, all of USPS's debt is issued by the Federal Financing Bank, a government corporation under the general supervision of the Secretary of the Treasury that was created by Congress in 1973 ().

[18] U.S. Postal Service, *FY2015 Report on Form 10-K*, p. 10.

[19] Federal Financing Bank, U.S. Department of the Treasury, *Financial Statements, September 30, 2015 and 2014 (With Independent Auditors' Reports Thereon),* November 10, 2015, pp. 2-3, at https://www.treasury.gov/ffb/financialstatements/Federal%20Financing%20Bank_Financial_Statements_FY2015_and_FY2014.pdf.

[20] Ibid.

[21] U.S. Postal Service, *FY2015 Report on Form 10-K*, pp. 49-50. Also see Federal Financing Bank, U.S. Department of the Treasury, *2015 Annual Report*, November 13, 2015, p. 4, at https://www.treasury.gov/ffb/ FFB%202015%20Annual%20Report.pdf#page=4.

[22] Ibid., p. 49.

[23] These prefunding obligations will be discussed in greater detail in the section of this report titled "Prefunding Requirement for Retiree Health Benefits."

[24] U.S. Postal Service, *FY2015 Report on Form 10-K*, p. 5.

25 This average is based on estimates from the PRC and the USPS. According to the PRC's calculation, the USPS had 24 days of operating cash in FY2015. See U.S. Postal Regulatory Commission, *Financial Analysis of United States Postal Service Financial Results and 10-K Statement, Fiscal Year 2015*, March 29, 2016, p. 33, at http://www.prc.gov/sites/default/ files/reports/FY%202015%20Financial%20Analysis%20Report.pdf. The USPS estimate, however, is 25 days, which is based on a slightly lower average operating cost per day ($270 million) than that used by the PRC ($275 million).

[26] At the end of FY2015, the USPS had total assets of $361.1 billion and total liabilities of $462.4 billion. U.S. Postal Service Board of Governors, *November 2015 Open Session Presentation*, p. 13, at http://about.usps.com/news/ electronic-press-kits/bog/open-session-151111.pdf.

[27] Title I, §101, 120 Stat. 3199.

[28] See sections of this report titled "Nonpostal Products and Services" and "Postal Banking."

[29.] For the full list of current market-dominant and competitive products, see U.S. Postal Regulatory Commission, *Mail Classification Schedule* (with revisions through April 10, 2016), *January 15, 2016*, at http://www.prc.gov/mailclassification-schedule.

[30] Ibid. Title IV, §401, 120 Stat. 3221. Title IV of the PAEA also mandates that competitive products not only cover the costs that are directly attributable to those products, but also cover a portion of the USPS's institutional costs, which are not attributable to any specific product.

[31] U.S. Postal Service, *FY2015 Report on Form 10-K*, p. 2. See **Table A-1** in **Appendix A** for additional data on USPS revenue and mail volume for FY2014 and FY2015.

[32] U.S. Postal Service, *Final Revenue, Pieces, and Weight by Classes of Mail and Special Services for Fiscal Year 2015*, October 2015, at http://about.usps.com/who-we-are/financials/revenue-pieces-weight-reports/fy2015-q4.csv.

[33] Average revenue per piece calculated using data from U.S. Postal Service, *Final Revenue, Pieces, and Weight by Classes of Mail and Special Services for Fiscal Year 2015*, October 2015, at http://about.usps.com/who-we-are/financials/revenue-pieces-weight-reports/fy 2015-q4.csv.

[34] U.S. Postal Service, *FY2014 Report on Form 10-K*, Washington, DC, 2014, p. 15, at http://about.usps.com/who-weare/financials/10k-reports/fy2014.pdf (hereafter, *FY2014 Report on Form 10-K*).

[35] U.S. Postal Service, *FY2014 Report on Form 10-K*, p. 15.

[36] Prior to implementation of the PAEA, the USPS did not report mail volume and revenue using the categories "competitive" and "market dominant." The FY2008 USPS financial reports were the first to utilize PAEA categories. In many instances, the FY2008 financial reports provided volume and revenue data for FY2007.

[37] The USPS's temporary price increase is discussed in greater detail in the section of this report titled "Exigent Price Increase".

[38] 39 U.S.C. §3622(d)(1)(E). The USPS has additional flexibility in establishing prices for competitive products. Their pricing decisions, however, are bound by market forces. For

example, if the USPS decides to increase rates by more than the market will bear, other firms may increase their market share relative to the USPS. Additionally, USPS must adhere to ratemaking procedures established by the PRC pursuant to the PAEA, such as publication of proposed rate changes in the *Federal Register*. 39 C.F.R. §3015.

39 When formulating regulations pursuant to the PAEA, the PRC considered and rejected defining *triggering events* or other circumstances that might qualify or disqualify as "extraordinary or exceptional". See U.S. Postal Regulatory Commission, *Regulations Establishing a System of Ratemaking: Order Establishing Ratemaking Regulations for Market Dominant and Competitive Products*, Docket No. RM2007-1, October 29, 2007, p. 65, at https://www.prc.gov/ docs/58/58026/FinalRuleswithTOC.pdf.

40 U.S. Postal Regulatory Commission, *Exigent Request of the United States Postal Service*, Docket No. R2010-4, July 6, 2010, at https://www.prc.gov/docs/68/68792/Request. Final.pdf.

41 Ibid., pp. 1-8.

42 U.S. Postal Regulatory Commission, *Order Denying Request for Exigent Price Adjustments*, Docket No. R2010-4, September 30, 2010, at https://www.prc.gov/Docs/70/70341/ Order_547.pdf.

43 U.S. Postal Regulatory Commission, *Order Granting Exigent Price Increase*, Docket No. R2013-11, December 24, 2013, at https://www.prc.gov/docs/88/88645/Order_1926.pdf.

44 Ibid., p. 193.

45 Ibid.

46 Ibid., p. 3.

47 Specifically, the USPS disagreed with (and the Court found "arbitrary and capricious") the PRC's "Count Once" rule. Under this rule, the PRC counted lost revenue from decreased mail volume for a maximum of 12 months, even in instances where the USPS argued it was likely that the volume loss exceeded 12 months.

For example, a worker laid off during the recession might cancel her cable subscription, and no longer pay her monthly bill by mail. The [PRC] would count that change as a loss of no more than twelve pieces of mail; the Postal Service would count it as lost volume for as long as the recession stands between that worker and her cable subscription. If it takes her four years to find a new job and resubscribe, the Postal Service would count forty-eight lost pieces of mail.

Alliance of Nonprofit Mailers, et al., v. Postal Regulatory Commission, (DC Cir. 2015). This opinion, found at http://www.cadc.uscourts.gov/internet/opinions.nsf/485AE8FFF47 BB70C85257E5B004F532A/$file/14-1009- 1555927.pdf, also provides a thorough review of the multi-step process that led to the PRC's approval of the exigent price increase and the subsequent legal challenges.

48 United States Postal Service, *FY2015 Report on Form 10-K*, pp. 2, 45.

49 Ibid. U.S. Postal Regulatory Commission, *Notice of the United States Postal Service of Removal of the Exigent Surcharge*, Docket No. R2013-11, February 26, 2016, at http://www.prc.gov/docs/95/95102/2016-02- 25%20Exigent%20Removal%20Notice.pdf. Also see the USPS Webinar on the exigent surcharge, at https://ribbs.usps.gov/mtac/ documents/tech_guides/webinararchives/2016Webinars/ExigentRollbackPriceChange Webinar.pdf.

50 Ibid.

51 Ibid.

52 U.S. Postal Regulatory Commission, Order on Revised Price Adjustments for Standard Mail, Periodicals, and Package Services Products and Related Mail Classification Changes,

Docket No. R2015-4, May 7, 2015, at http://www.prc.gov/docs/92/92217/Order%20 No.%202472.pdf.

[53] Within this report, *operating expenses* excludes (1) the statutorily required payments to prefund health benefits for future retirees, which are discussed in the "Prefunding Requirement for Retiree Health Benefits section of this report; (2) workers' compensation non-cash adjustments; and (3) supplemental payments to the Federal Employees' Retirement System (FERS) required due to a revaluation of USPS's retiree liability. In FY2015, these expenses were about $6.2 billion. U.S. Postal Regulatory Commission, *Financial Analysis of United States Postal Service Financial Results and 10-K Statement, Fiscal Year 2015,* March 29, 2016, pp. 10-12, at http://www.prc.gov/sites/default/files/ reports/FY%202015%20Financial%20Analysis%20Report.pdf; U.S. Postal Service, *FY2015 Report on Form 10-K*, p. 22.

[54] U.S. Postal Service, *FY2015 Report on Form 10-K*, pp. 14-19.

[55] U.S. Postal Service, *FY2015 Report on Form 10-K*, p. 19.

[56] U.S. Postal Regulatory Commission, *Financial Analysis of United States Postal Service Financial Results and 10-K Statement, Fiscal Year 2015,* March 29, 2016, pp. 11-12.

[57] *Salaries* includes full-time and part-time employees and other costs, such as performance awards.

[58] U.S. Postal Service, *Reports on Form 10-K (2012-2015)*, Washington, DC, 2015, available at http://about.usps.com/ who-we-are/financials/welcome.htm.

[59] U.S. Postal Service, *FY2015 Report on Form 10-K*, p. 19.

[60] U.S. Postal Service, *Reports on Form 10-K (2012-2015)*, Washington, DC, 2015, available at http://about.usps.com/ who-we-are/financials/welcome.htm.

[61] U.S. Postal Service, Office of the Inspector General, *Peeling the Onion: The Real Cost of Mail,* April 18, 2016, RARC-WP-16-009, pp. 13-14, at https://www.uspsoig.gov/sites/ default/files/document-library-files/2016/RARC-WP16-009.pdf. For information on transportation contracts, see U.S. Postal Service, *Procurement Manual*, Chapter 12 "Mail Transportation," July 12, 1995, at http://about.usps.com/ publications/pub41/pub41c12.pdf.

[62] 39 U.S.C. §2005(a)(2)(C).

[63] U.S. Postal Service, *FY2015 Report on Form 10-K*, p. 10.

[64] For questions about the prefunding requirement, contact Annie L. Mach, Specialist in Health Care Financing (7 7825).

[65] For additional details on the prefunding requirement and issues related to USPS pension funding, see CRS Report R43349, *U.S. Postal Service Retiree Health Benefits and Pension Funding Issues*, by Katelin P. Isaacs and Annie L. Mach.

[66] Congress deferred the FY2011 payment until FY2012 ().

[67] In its *FY2015 Report on Form 10-K,* the USPS indicates that it will likely default on the FY2016 payment.

[68] U.S. Postal Service, *FY2015 Report on Form 10-K*, p. 32.

[69] U.S. Postal Service, *FY2015 Report on Form 10-K*, p. 5.

[70] U.S. Postal Service, *FY2015 Report on Form 10-K*, p. 32.

[71] This section authored by Kathryn A. Francis, Analyst in Government Organization and Management (7-2351).

[72] U.S. Postal Service, *FY2014 Report on the Form 10-K*, p. 20.

[73] CRS analysis of U.S. Postal Service *FY2014 Report on the Form 10-K*, and U.S. Postal Service, *2014 Annual Report to Congress*, December 31, 2014, p. 68, at https://about.usps.com/publications/annual-report-comprehensive-statement2014/welcome-landing.htm.

[74] USPS has utilized the Voluntary Early Retirement Authority (VERA) and Voluntary Separation Incentive Program (VSIP). For more information on the VERA, see 5 U.S.C. §8336(d)(2)(D), 5 U.S.C. §8414(b)(1)(B), 5 C.F.R. §831.114, 5 C.F.R. §842.213, and OPM, *Guide To Voluntary Early Retirement Regulations,* August 2006, at https://www.opm.gov/policy-data-oversight/workforce-restructuring/voluntary-early-retirement-authority/ vera_guide.pdf. For more information on the VSIP, see 5 U.S.C. §3521, 5 C.F.R. part 576, and OPM, *Guide to Voluntary Separation Incentive Payments,* August 2006, at https://www.opm.gov/policy-data-oversight/workforcerestructuring/ voluntary-separation-incentive-payments/guide.pdf.

[75] See sections titled "Restructuring the Processing and Delivery Network" and "Retail Post Office Closures"; U.S. Postal Service Office of the Inspector General (hereafter USPS OIG), *Management Advisory Report, Lessons Learned from Mail Processing Network Rationalization Initiatives*, March 27, 2013, p. 4, at https://www.uspsoig.gov/ sites/default/files/document-library-files/2013/no-ma-13-004.pdf; U.S. Postal Service, "POStPlan Org Change/RIF Timeline," at http://www.postmasters.org/ News/PostPlan/ POStPLAN%20RIF%20Timeline.pdf.

[76] For more information on reductions-in-force, see 5 U.S.C. §3501-3503, and 5 C.F.R. Part 351.

[77] Electronic correspondence with USPS staff on June 8, 2015. For more information on Discontinued Service Retirement, see 5 U.S.C. §8336(d) and 5 C.F.R. §831.503.

[78] Electronic correspondence with USPS staff on June 8, 2015.

[79] For a list of benefits provided to USPS career employees, see U.S. Postal Service, "Compensation and Benefits," at https://about.usps.com/careers/working-usps/benefits.htm.

[80] U.S. Postal Service, *Employee and Labor Relations Manual*, ELM 36, September 2013, p. 572, at http://about.usps.com/manuals/elm/elmc5.pdf.

[81] CRS analysis of U.S. Postal Service *Reports on the Form 10-K*, and U.S. Postal Service, *Annual Reports to Congress*.

[82] CRS analysis of U.S. Postal Service, *Annual Reports to Congress*. For more detailed information on trends in USPS career and non-career employees, see CRS Report RS22864, *U.S. Postal Service Workforce Size and Employment Categories, FY1995-FY2014*, by Kathryn A. Francis.

[83] CRS analysis of U.S. Postal Service *Reports on the Form 10-K*.

[84] For an example of the intended goals of Mail Handler Assistants, see National Postal Mail Handlers Union, and U.S. Postal Service, *Board of Interest Arbitration Award*, February 15, 2013, pp. 12, at http://www.npmhu.org/resources/document/20130215-Final-NPMHU_ USPS-Interest-Arbitration-Award.pdf.

[85] National Association of Letter Carriers (hereafter NALC) and USPS, *2011-2016 National Agreement,* p. 28, at http://www.nalc.org/member-benefits/body/na2011.pdf. See GAO, *U.S. Postal Service, Status of Workforce Reductions and Related Planning Efforts*, GAO-15-43, November 13 2014, p. 18, at http://www.gao.gov/assets/670/666884.pdf.

[86] USPS OIG, *Use of Non-Traditional Full-Time and Postal Support Employee Positions in Processing Operations,* Report Number NO-AR-13-003, May 17, 2013, p. 5, at https://www.uspsoig.gov/sites/default/files/document-libraryfiles/2013/no-ar-13-003.pdf.

[87] U.S. Postal Service, *FY2014 Report on the Form 10-K*, p. 20; U.S. Postal Regulatory Commission, *Financial Analysis of United States Postal Service Financial Results and 10-K Statement, Fiscal Year 2014,* April 1, 2015, p. 12. Total compensation does not include retirement, health benefits, workers' compensation, or RHBF payments.

[88] U.S. Postal Regulatory Commission, *Financial Analysis of United States Postal Service Financial Results and 10-K Statement, Fiscal Year 2014,* April 1, 2015, pp. 13-14. For a

definition of productive hourly wage rate, see U.S. Postal Regulatory Commission, "Notice of the USPS and Further Revised Response of Witness Colvin to Greeting Card Association Interrogatory GSA/USPS-T7-1," July 19, 2010, p. 3, at http://www.prc.gov/docs/69/69174/REVISED.GCA.1.Jul.19.pdf.

[89] U.S. Postal Regulatory Commission, *Financial Analysis of United States Postal Service Financial Results and 10-K Statement, Fiscal Year 2014,* April 1, 2015, p. 12.

[90] U.S. Postal Service, Office of the Inspector General, *Peeling the Onion: The Real Cost of Mail,* April 18, 2016, RARC-WP-16-009, pp. 10-11, at https://www.uspsoig.gov/sites/default/files/document-library-files/2016/RARC-WP16-009.pdf.

[91] Government Accountability Office, *U.S. Postal Service, Status of Workforce Reductions and Related Planning Efforts*, GAO-15-43, November 13 2014. The GAO report includes initiatives that are not discussed in this report.

[92] Ibid., pp. 9-10.

[93] Ibid., pp. 10-11.

[94] Ibid., p. 11.

[95] This section authored by Michelle D. Christensen (7-0764).

[96] U.S. Postal Service, *Five-Year Business Plan*, April 16, 2013, at http://about.usps.com/strategic-planning/fiveyearplan-04162013-final.pdf.

[97] Ibid., pp. 15-17.

[98] Ibid., pp. 15-19.

[99] This section authored by Michelle D. Christensen (7-0764).

[100] See U.S. Postal Service, "Our Future Network: USPS Delivery Standards and Statistics Fact Sheet," at http://about.usps.com/news/electronic-press-kits/our-future-network/ofn-usps-delivery-standards-and-statistics-factsheet.htm.

[101] The new revised standards went into effect on January 5, 2015, and are available at 39 C.F.R. §121. Also see U.S. Postal Service, *Five-Year Business Plan*, April 16, 2013, pp. 15-19, at http://about.usps.com/strategic-planning/ fiveyearplan-04162013-final.pdf.

[102] 39 C.F.R. §121, Appendix A.

[103] Specifically, prior to January 5, 2015, with certain exceptions, an overnight service standard applied to First-Class mail that was received and was being delivered within an area served by a single U.S. Postal Service Sectional Center Facility (i.e., postal processing and distribution facility), provided the mail arrived at the facility by a certain time (referred to as the "critical entry time" or CET). After January 5, for First-Class mail to be subject to overnight business rules, it must be "Presort" mail (i.e., sorted and containerized by Zip code by the mailer). For additional details, see summary and comments accompanying the Final Rule, "Revised Service Standards for Market-Dominant Mail Products," at http://about.usps.com/news/facility-studies/_pdf/market-dominant-final-rule.pdf.

[104] U.S. Postal Regulatory Commission, *Annual Compliance Determination Report FY2015*, March 28, 2016, pp. 133 135, at http://www.prc.gov/sites/default/files/reports/Final_2015_ACD.pdf.

[105] This section authored by Michelle D. Christensen (7-0764).

[106] See U.S. Postal Service, "Our Future Network: Phase 2 Network Rationalization Frequently Asked Questions," at http://about.usps.com/news/electronic-press-kits/our-future-network/ofn-phase-2-faqs-new.htm.

[107] Ibid. Also see U.S. Postal Service, *Five-Year Business Plan*, April 16, 2013, pp. 15-19, at http://about.usps.com/ strategic-planning/fiveyearplan-04162013-final.pdf.

[108] While several bills have been introduced in the 113th and 114th Congresses that would have placed restrictions on the closure of postal facilities, none have been enacted. See, for example, (113th), (113th), and (114th).

[109] U.S. Postal Regulatory Commission, *Response of the United States Postal Service to Question 16 of Chairman's Information Request No. 7*, Docket No. ACR2015, February 11, 2016, p. 2, at http://www.prc.gov/docs/94/94968/CHIR_No_7.Second.Response.Set. Q16.pdf.

[110] Ibid.

[111] Ibid.

[112] Ibid.

[113] U.S. Postal Service, Office of the Inspector General, *Peeling the Onion: The Real Cost of Mail,* April 18, 2016, RARC-WP-16-009, p. 13, at https://www.uspsoig.gov/sites/default/files/document-library-files/2016/RARC-WP-16- 009.pdf.

[114] U.S. Postal Service, Office of the Inspector General, *Management Alert – Substantial Increase in Delayed Mail,* Report Number NO-MA-15-004, August 13, 2015, at https://www.uspsoig.gov/sites/default/files/document-libraryfiles/2015/no-ma-15-004.pdf.

[115] Ibid., p 3.

[116] Ibid., pp. 3-5.

[117] Ibid.

[118] This section authored by Michelle D. Christensen (7-0764). For additional background on the history of six-day delivery, see CRS Report R40626, *The U.S. Postal Service and Six-Day Delivery: History, Issues, and Current Legislation*, by Wendy Ginsberg.

[119] For example, in the USPS's *Business Plan*, section titled "Executing on Identified Initiatives is Core to Addressing USPS's Financial Challenges," the USPS recommended adjusting service levels to six-day delivery of packages and five-day delivery of first-class mail. U.S. Postal Service, *Five-Year Business Plan*, April 16, 2013, p. 17, at http://about.usps.com/strategic-planning/fiveyearplan-04162013-final.pdf#page=17.

[120] The Postal Service has offered seven-day package delivery in select regions during the holiday shipping season. It has also entered into negotiated service agreements with large shippers (e.g., Amazon) to offer Sunday delivery from select hubs across the United States. U.S. Postal Service, "Postal Service to Delivery Packages Seven Days a Week During Holidays," November 6, 2014, http://about.usps.com/news/national-releases/2014/pr14_057.htm; U.S. Postal Service Office of Inspector General, *Sunday Parcel Delivery Service: Audit Report*, December 5, 2014, https://www.uspsoig.gov/sites/default/files/document-library-files/2015/dr-ar-15-002.pdf.

[121] U.S. Postal Regulatory Commission, *Annual Compliance Determination Report FY2015*, March 28, 2016, p. 3, http://www.prc.gov/sites/default/files/reports/Final_2015_ACD.pdf; U.S. Postal Regulatory Commission, *Analysis of FY 2015 Performance Report and FY 2016 Performance Plan*, May 4, 2016, p. 2, at http://www.prc.gov/sites/default/files/reports/Appendix%20-%20Findings%20and%20Recommdations.pdf.

[122] Urs Trinkner and Andreas Haller, *Impact of Discontinuance of Saturday Delivery for Letters and Flats*, Swiss Economics for the U.S. Postal Regulatory Commission, ISSN 2235-1868, February 2014, pp. 7-8, at http://www.prc.gov/sites/default/files/reports/FinalReport.pdf.

[123] Ibid., pp. 8-9.

[124] Ibid.

[125] Ibid., p. 9.

[126] This section coauthored by Michelle D. Christensen (7-0764) and Kathryn A. Francis (7-2351).

[127] The list of POStPlan facilities is available at http://about.usps.com/news/electronic-press-kits/our-future-network/ assets/pdf/postplan-affected-post-offices-120509.pdf.

[128] For descriptions of the categories and types of postal facilities, please see CRS Report R41950, *The U.S. Postal Service: Common Questions About Post Office Closures*, by Michelle D. Christensen.

[129] U.S. Postal Regulatory Commission, *Financial Analysis of United States Postal Service Financial Results and 10-K Statement, Fiscal Year 2014, April 1, 2015,* p. 14, at http://www.prc.gov/sites/default/files/reports/ Financial%20Report%202014.pdf; and Government Accountability Office, *U.S. Postal Service, Status of Workforce Reductions and Related Planning Efforts*, GAO-15-43, November 13 2014, pp. 14-16. The GAO report did not specify the position types that experienced reduced work hours.

[130] Government Accountability Office, *U.S. Postal Service, Status of Workforce Reductions and Related Planning Efforts*, GAO-15-43, November 13, 2014, p. 13.

[131] Ibid., pp. 14-20.

[132] This section authored by Kathryn A. Francis (7-2351).

[133] U.S. Postal Service, *Five Year Business Plan*, April 2013, p. 28, at http://about.usps.com/strategic-planning/ fiveyearplan-04162013-final.pdf. The USPS anticipates a reduction of approximately 146,000 career and non-career full-time equivalents by 2017.

[134] Ibid., CRS analysis of U.S. Postal Service *Reports on the Form 10-K.*

[135] Government Accountability Office, *U.S. Postal Service, Status of Workforce Reductions and Related Planning Efforts*, GAO-15-43, November 13 2014, p. 13.

[136] U.S. Postal Service, "Phase 2 Network Rationalization," p. 1, at https://about.usps.com/news/electronic-press-kits/ our-future-network/assets/pdf/ofn-phase-2-faqs.pdf.

[137] American Postal Workers Union, "APWU Wins Major Victory on Staffing 'POStPlan' Offices," September 22, 2014, at http://www.apwu.org/news/web-news-article/apwu-wins-major-victory-staffing%E2%80%98postplan%E2%80%99-offices.

[138] National Association of Letter Carriers and U.S. Postal Service, *2011-2016 National Agreement*, p. 16.

[139] National Association of Letter Carriers and U.S. Postal Service, *2006-2011 National Agreement,* p. 15, at http://www.nalc.org/workplace-issues/contract-administration-unit/body/na2006.pdf. The 2006 agreement places limitations on the number of "transitional employees," a non-career employee category that was phased out and replaced by CCAs in 2013.

[140] National Association of Letter Carriers and U.S. Postal Service, *2011-2016 National Agreement*, p. 16.

[141] American Postal Workers Union, "USPS Demands Cuts in Pay, Benefits, Job Security," May 28, 2015, at http://www.apwu.org/news/news-bulletin/usps-demands-cuts-pay-benefits-job-security.

[142] Ibid.

[143] Ibid.

[144] American Postal Workers Union and U.S. Postal Service, *2015 National Agreement, Interest Arbitration Decision and Award*, July 8, 2016, p. 23, at http://www.apwu.org/sites/apwu/files/resource-files/7.08.16.%20FINAL%20AWARD.2015%20NATIONAL%20AGREEMENT%20signed.pdf.

[145] Government Accountability Office, *U.S. Postal Service, Status of Workforce Reductions and Related Planning Efforts*, GAO-15-43, November 13 2014, p. 18.

[146] American Postal Workers Union, "Management and Privatizers: Reading From the Same Script," at http://www.apwu.org/news/deptdiv-news-article/management-and-privatizers-reading-same-script.

[147] Letter from Senator Heidi Heitkamp, United States Senate, to Patrick Donahoe, former Postmaster General, March 5, 2014, PDF pp. 2-3, at http://www.heitkamp.senate.gov/public/_cache/files/4783d5ff-7e49-4d6b-868a-6df7bc3bee74/postmaster-general-nd-postal-service-letter.pdf.

[148] (114th Congress).

[149] Under §6(c)(1) of, "the Chief Morale Officer must have, among other things, experience 'revitalizing and improving the morale' of entities that have experienced financial or other challenges."

[150] The term *national initiatives* is not further defined in the bill.

[151] Ibid.

[152] For additional details, see **Table B-1** in **Appendix B**.

[153] This section authored by Garrett Hatch, Specialist in American National Government (7-7822).

[154] U.S. Postal Service, *Delivering the Mail and More: Postal Service Mission and "Motto"*, at https://about.usps.com/ who-we-are/postal-history/mission-motto.pdf.

[155] U.S. Postal Service, Office of Inspector General, *The Road to a New Delivery Fleet*, July 28, 2014, at https://www.uspsoig.gov/blog/road-new-delivery-fleet.

[156] U.S. Postal Service, *FY2015 Integrated Financial Plan*, p. 3, at https://about.usps.com/who-we-are/financials/ integrated-financial-plans/fy2015.pdf.

[157] Government Accountability Office, *Federal Vehicle Fleets: Leading Practices for Managing Fleet Operations*, GAO-15-644T, p. 4, at http://www.gao.gov/assets/680/670331.pdf.

[158] U.S. Postal Service, Office of Inspector General, *The Road to a New Delivery Fleet*, July 28, 2014.

[159] Testimony of U.S. Postal Service Chief Financial Officer and Executive Vice President, Joseph Corbett, in U.S. Congress, House Committee on Oversight and Government Reform, Subcommittee on Government Operations, *Issues Facing Civilian and Postal Service Vehicle Procurement*, hearings, 114th Cong., 1st sess., May 21, 2015, at http://docs.house.gov/meetings/GO/GO24/20150521/103521/HHRG-114-GO24-Wstate-CorbettJ-20150521.pdf.

[160] U.S. Postal Service, *Request for Information and Prequalification/Sources Sought for Next Generation Delivery Vehicle (NGDV) Acquisition Program*, January 20, 2015, p. 5, at https://www.fbo.gov/index?s=opportunity&mode=form&tab=core&id=e4c65069740a6b4df5158fb0a9512b1c&_cview=0.

[161] Testimony of U.S. Postal Service Chief Financial Officer and Executive Vice President, Joseph Corbett, in U.S. Congress, House Committee on Oversight and Government Reform, Subcommittee on Government Operations, *Issues Facing Civilian and Postal Service Vehicle Procurement*, hearings, 114th Cong., 1st sess., May 21, 2015.

[162] U.S. Postal Service, Office of Inspector General, *Delivery Vehicle Fleet Replacement*, DR-MA-14-005, June 10, 2014, p. 4, at https://www.uspsoig.gov/sites/default/files/document-library-files/2014/dr-ma-14-005.pdf.

[163] U.S. Postal Service, *Request for Information and Prequalification/Sources Sought for Next Generation Delivery Vehicle (NGDV) Acquisition Program*, January 20, 2015, p. 5, at https://www.fbo.gov/index?s=opportunity&mode=form&tab=core&id=e4c65069740a6b4df5158fb0a9512b1c&_cview=0.

[164] Ibid., pp. 1,5.

[165] Ibid.

[166] U.S. Postal Service, Office of Inspector General, *The Road to a New Delivery Fleet*, July 28, 2014.

[167] U.S. Postal Service, *Request for Information and Prequalification/Sources Sought for Next Generation Delivery Vehicle (NGDV) Acquisition Program*, January 20, 2015, p. 1, at https://www.fbo.gov/index?s=opportunity&mode=form&tab=core&id=e4c65069740 a6b4df5158fb0a9512b1c&_cview=0.

[168] Ibid., p.5.

[169] U.S. Postal Service, *Next Generation Delivery Vehicle (NGDV) Acquisition Program-Prequalified Sources*, April 14, 2015, p. 1, at https://www.fbo.gov/utils/ view?id=62fddc4 fa87e8c3de4436a631e715a51.

[170] U.S. Postal Service, *Request for Information and Prequalification/Sources Sought for Next Generation Delivery Vehicle (NGDV) Acquisition Program*, January 20, 2015, p. 3, at https://www.fbo.gov/index?s=opportunity&mode=form&tab=core&id=e4c65069740 a6b4df5158fb0a9512b1c&_cview=0.

[171] U.S. Postal Service, *Next Generation Delivery Vehicle (NGDV) Prototype Request for Proposal (RFP): Statement of Objectives* (Attachment 1), October 20, 2015, p. 2, at https://www.fbo.gov/utils/view?id= e5b5d2b386ee44c694aff2c5f2900c8f.

[172] Testimony of U.S. Postal Service Chief Financial Officer and Executive Vice President, Joseph Corbett, in U.S. Congress, House Committee on Oversight and Government Reform, Subcommittee on Government Operations, *Issues Facing Civilian and Postal Service Vehicle Procurement*, hearings, 114th Cong., 1st sess., May 21, 2015.

[173] Ibid.

[174] Ibid.

[175] This section authored by Michelle D. Christensen (7-0764).

[176] P.L. 109-435, Title I, §§101-102, 120 Stat. 3199. Regulations subsequently issued by the PRC state that a *postal service* "refers to the delivery of letters, printed matter, or mailable packages, including acceptance, collection, sorting, transportation, or other functions ancillary thereto" and that a *postal product* "means a postal service with a distinct cost or market characteristic for which a rate or rates are, or may reasonably be, applied." 39 C.F.R. §§3001.5(s)-(t).

[177] Ibid.

[178] U.S. Postal Regulatory Commission, *Order Approving Mail Classification Schedule Descriptions and Prices for Nonpostal Service Products*, Docket No. MC2010-24, December 11, 2012.

[179] U.S. Postal Regulatory Commission, *Mail Classification Schedule*, January 15, 2016, pp. 203-204, at http://www.prc.gov/mail-classification-schedule; U.S. Government Accountability Office, *U.S. Postal Service: Overview of Initiatives to Increase Revenue and Introduce Nonpostal Services and Experimental Postal Products*, January 2013, p. 18, at http://www.gao.gov/assets/660/651298.pdf.

[180] U.S. Postal Regulatory Commission, *Mail Classification Schedule*, January 15, 2016, p. 204. Also see U.S. Postal Service retail website, "Stamp Collector Zone," at https://store.usps.com/store/browse/subcategory.jsp?categoryId=stamp-collectors&category NavIds=stamp-collectors.

[181] U.S. Postal Regulatory Commission, *Mail Classification Schedule*, January 15, 2016, p. 538. Also see U.S. Government Accountability Office, *U.S. Postal Service: Overview of Initiatives to Increase Revenue and Introduce Nonpostal Services and Experimental Postal Products*, January 2013, pp. 18-20.

[182] Ibid., p. 537.
[183] Ibid., p. 538.
[184] Ibid., p. 539.
[185] Ibid., p. 540.
[186] Ibid., p. 541.
[187] Ibid., p. 542.
[188] Ibid., p. 543.
[189] Ibid., p. 544.
[190] U.S. Postal Regulatory Commission, *Annual Compliance Determination Report FY2015*, March 28, 2016, p. 75, at http://www.prc.gov/sites/default/files/reports/Final_2015_ACD.pdf.
[191] Ibid., p. 92.
[192] Ibid., pp. 75, 92.
[193] 39 U.S.C. §3641; 39 C.F.R. §3503.
[194] U.S. Postal Regulatory Commission, "Market Test Dockets," at http://www.prc.gov/dockets/type/MarketTest. See dockets MT 2011-2; MT 2013-1; and MT 2016-1. Also see U.S. Postal Service "Metro Post" at https://www.usps.com/ metropost.
[195] U.S. Postal Service Office of Inspector General, *OIG Blog: Ideas Worth Exploring*, "Groceries to Your Door," June 27, 2016, at https://www.uspsoig.gov/blog/groceries-your-door.
[196] (113th); (113th); (113th); (114th); (114th).
[197] (113th); (113th).
[198] Ibid.
[199] Ibid.
[200] (113th); (113th); (113th); (113th); (114th); (114th).
[201] The two bills use different criteria and procedures to determine which nonpostal products and services the USPS would be permitted to offer. For additional details, see S. 2051, §303; and H.R. 5714, §204.
[202] This section authored by Michelle D. Christensen (7-0764) and Daniel J. Richardson, former Research Assistant at CRS. The terms *Postal Banking* and *Postal Financial Services* are used interchangeably in this section.
[203] In 1910, Congress passed "An Act to establish postal savings depositories," (36 Stat. 814). The postal savings system was discontinued in 1966 by P.L. 89-377; 80 Stat. 92. Pursuant to the *Postal Savings System Statute of Limitations Act* (; 98 Stat. 402), any money that remained in postal savings accounts as of July 13, 1985, was retained by the U.S. Treasury and could no longer be claimed by the depositors. All unclaimed funds were transferred to the Treasury-managed account "Unclaimed Moneys of Individuals Whose Whereabouts Are Unknown," and, with certain exceptions, will be held in perpetuity. 31 U.S.C. §1322.
[204] According to a 2009 journal article on Japan's postal banking system, at least 18 countries have established some form of postal banking, though not all are still operational today: United Kingdom (established 1861), New Zealand (established 1867), Canada (established 1868), Belgium (established 1870), Japan (established 1875), Italy (established 1876), France (established 1881), the Netherlands (established 1881), Austria (established 1883), Sweden (established 1884), Finland (established 1887), Greece (established 1902), the United States (established 1910), Spain (established 1916), Ireland (established 1923), Germany (established 1939), Norway (established 1950), and Denmark (established 1991). See Masami Imai, "Ideologies, Vested Interest Groups, and Postal Saving Privatization in Japan," *Public Choice*, vol. 138, no. 1/2 (January 2009), p. 139.

205 Murthy M L N and Vani Vangala, *Bank@Post Office- A Global Trend: Thought Paper*, Infosys Finacle, Bangalore, India, at http://www.infosys.com/finacle/solutions/thought-papers/Documents/bank@post-office-global-trend.pdf. This paper includes a review of various models currently used around the world, pp. 3-4.

206 U.S. Postal Service, Office of the Inspector General, *Providing Non-Bank Financial Services for the Underserved*, RARC-WP-14-007, Arlington, VA, January 27, 2014, at https://uspsoig.gov/sites/default/files/document-library-files/ 2014/rarc-wp-14-007.pdf.

207 U.S. Postal Service, Office of the Inspector General, *The Road Ahead for Postal Financial Services*, RARC-WP-15- 011, Arlington, VA, May 10, 2015, at https://uspsoig.gov/sites/default/files/document-library-files/2015/rarc-wp-15- 011.pdf.

208 Ibid/, p. 16.

209 Ibid., pp. 18-24.

210 Ibid., p. 10 offers a comparison of each of the five approaches, compared on potential revenue, cost, benefits to the underserved, and operational complexity.

211 The FDIC primer on alternative financial services states that this term is "often used to describe the array of financial services offered by providers that operate outside of federally insured banks and thrifts (hereafter referred to as "banks"). Check-cashing outlets, money transmitters, car title lenders, payday loan stores, pawnshops, and rent-toown stores are all considered AFS providers. However, many of the products and services they provide are not "alternative"; rather, they are the same as or similar to those offered by banks." Christine Bradley, Susan Burhouse, and Heather Gratton, et al., *Alternative Financial Services: A Primer*, Federal Deposit Insurance Corporation, April 27, 2009, at https://www.fdic.gov/bank/analytical/quarterly/2009_vol3_1/AltFinServicesprimer.html.

212 Susan Burhouse, Karyen Chu, and Ryan Goodstein, et al., *2013 FDIC National Survey of Unbanked and Underbanked Households: Executive Summary*, Federal Deposit Insurance Commission, October 2014, at https://www.fdic.gov/householdsurvey/2013execsumm.pdf.

213 See both Kevin R. Kosar, "Return to Sender: Postal banking is an idea whose time has come-and gone," *The Weekly Standard*, June 22, 2015, at http://www.weeklystandard.com/ articles/return-sender_969654.html, and Kevin Drum, "The Case Against Postal Banking," *Mother Jones*, November 12, 2014, at http://www.motherjones.com/kevin-drum/ 2014/11/case-against-postal-banking, for examples of this critique.

214 Charles Lane, "Postal Banking Could Make the Postal System's Troubles Worse," *Washington Post, Opinions*, April 1, 2015, at https://www.washingtonpost.com/ opinions/postal-banking-could-make-the-postal-systems-troubles-worse/2015/04/01/ad1c643c-d88b-11e4-b3f2-607bd612aeac_story.html.

215 U.S. Congress, House Committee on Post Office and Civil Service, *Discontinuance of Postal Savings System*, Report to accompany, 89th Cong., 1st sess., June 9, 1965, H. Rept. 89-483 (Washington: GPO, 1965).

216 (113th).

217 The white paper by the USPS OIG examines the costs, risks, and potential benefits of five options for expanding postal financial services ranging from (1) expansion of financial products USPS currently offers to (5) a development of a fully chartered and licensed bank. U.S. Postal Service, Office of the Inspector General, *The Road Ahead for Postal Financial Services*, RARC-WP-15-011, Arlington, VA, May 10, 2015, at https://uspsoig.gov/sites/default/files/ document-library-files/2015/rarc-wp-15-011.pdf.

218 Ibid.

[219] A similar bill, H.R. 5179 (113th), was introduced by Representative Richmond in the 113th Congress. For additional details, see Table B-1 in Appendix B.

[220] (114th). The bill uses the definition of *depository institutions* provided in the Federal Deposit Insurance Act (12 U.S.C. §1813), which is "any bank or savings association."

In: U.S. Postal Service Reform
Editor: Martin Thomas
ISBN: 978-1-53610-463-9

Chapter 2

U.S. POSTAL SERVICE WORKFORCE SIZE AND EMPLOYMENT CATEGORIES, FY1995-FY2014*

Kathryn A. Francis

SUMMARY

This report provides data from the past 20 years on the size and composition of the U.S. Postal Service's (USPS's) workforce. Reforms to the size and composition of the workforce have been an integral part of USPS's strategy to reduce costs and regain financial solvency, particularly between FY2007 and FY2014. Since 2007, USPS has experienced significant revenue losses that have affected its ability to manage its expenses. Personnel costs are one of the primary drivers of USPS's operating expenses. As such, USPS has employed strategies to reform the size and composition of its workforce in an effort to cut personnel costs, primarily through attrition and separation incentives and increased use of lower-cost employees. These strategies reduced personnel expenses between FY2013 and FY2014. The sustainability of these reduced expenses and their overall impact on USPS's ability to regain financial solvency, however, is unclear.

The size of the USPS workforce has declined in the past 20 years. The number of employees has dropped by 257,095 (29.4%) in the past 20

* This is an edited, reformatted and augmented version of a Congressional Research Service publication, RS22864, dated October 21, 2015.

years, from 874,972 in FY1995 to 617,877 in FY2014. USPS, however, had 163 more employees at the end of FY2014 than it did at the end of FY2013. Declines in workforce size between FY2010 and FY2014 were driven, in part, by USPS's efforts to reduce its workforce size through attrition and separation incentives. Between FY2010 and FY2014, 55,473 career employees accepted a separation incentive to retire or resign early. On January 9, 2015, USPS instituted a reduction in force for 249 postmasters who did not accept a separation incentive offered in 2014.

The composition of USPS's workforce has also changed over the past two decades. USPS categorizes its workforce into two types of employees: career and non-career. Career employees serve in permanent positions on a full-time or part-time basis and typically receive full federal benefits. Non-career employees serve in time-limited or otherwise temporary positions and can often perform the full range of duties of career counterparts at lower wage rates, which might lower personnel costs.

USPS has increased the number of non-career employees in an effort to reduce personnel costs, particularly since FY2011. Between FY2011and FY2014, the number of non-career employees increased by 46.1%, from 88,699 to 129,577 employees. The influx in non-career employees since FY2011 is primarily attributable to the establishment of three new non-career positions: postal support employees, city carrier assistants, and mail handler assistants. Labor union contracts governing these positions, which went into effect in 2011 and 2013, effectively raised the total number of non-career employees that can comprise the USPS workforce. Career employees, however, continued to comprise the majority of the total workforce in FY2014 (79%).

BACKGROUND

The purpose of this report is to provide data on the size and composition of USPS's workforce between FY1995 and FY2014.[1] Reforms to the size and composition of the workforce have been an integral part of USPS's strategy to reduce costs and regain financial solvency, particularly after the onset of substantial revenue losses in FY2007. Historical context on USPS's workforce size and composition is therefore useful to understanding the magnitude of these workforce reforms and their impact on USPS's financial condition.

USPS WORKFORCE SIZE AND COMPOSITION

Workforce Size

Between FY1995 and FY2014, the size of USPS's workforce decreased 29.4%, from 874,972 employees to 617,877 employees (*Table 2*). Data on the overall workforce during this 20-year period show a rise in employees in the 1990s and a decline in employees from the 2000s through the present. During this time, USPS's workforce peaked in FY1999 with 905,766 employees. The USPS workforce experienced the steepest decrease in the past two decades between FY2008 and FY2009—a decrease of 53,006 employees, or 7.4% of the overall workforce. It can be noted that the Great Recession occurred between these years, which might have contributed to the decrease.[2] In FY2013, USPS operated with its smallest workforce in at least 20 years (*Figure 1*).

FY1995-FY2014

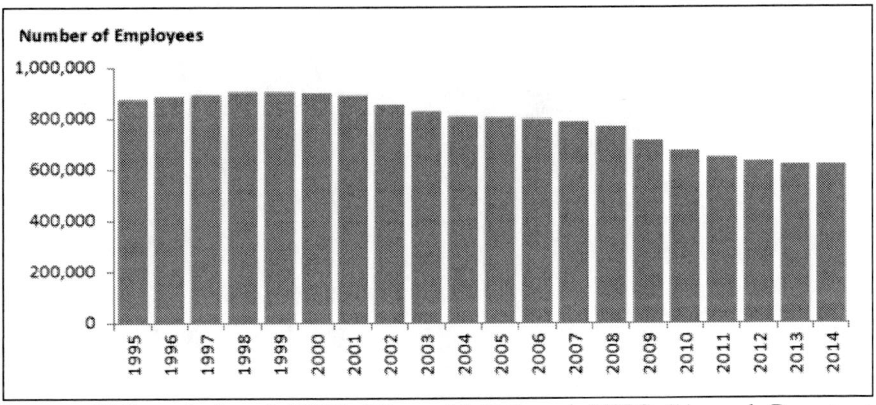

Source: CRS analysis of USPS "Form 10-Ks" and USPS "Annual Reports to Congress."

Figure 1. Total Number of U.S. Postal Service Employees.

Employment Trends: Career and Non-Career Employees

USPS categorizes its workforce into two types of employees: career and non-career. [3] Career employees serve in permanent positions on a full-time or part-time basis and typically receive full federal benefits.[4] Non-career employees, in contrast, serve in time-limited or otherwise temporary positions on a full-time or part-time basis. In many cases, non-career employees earn lower wages and are not provided benefits that are provided to career employees. For example, non-career employees are not eligible for federal life insurance and are not covered under the Federal Employees Retirement System (FERS).[5]

As of September 30, 2014

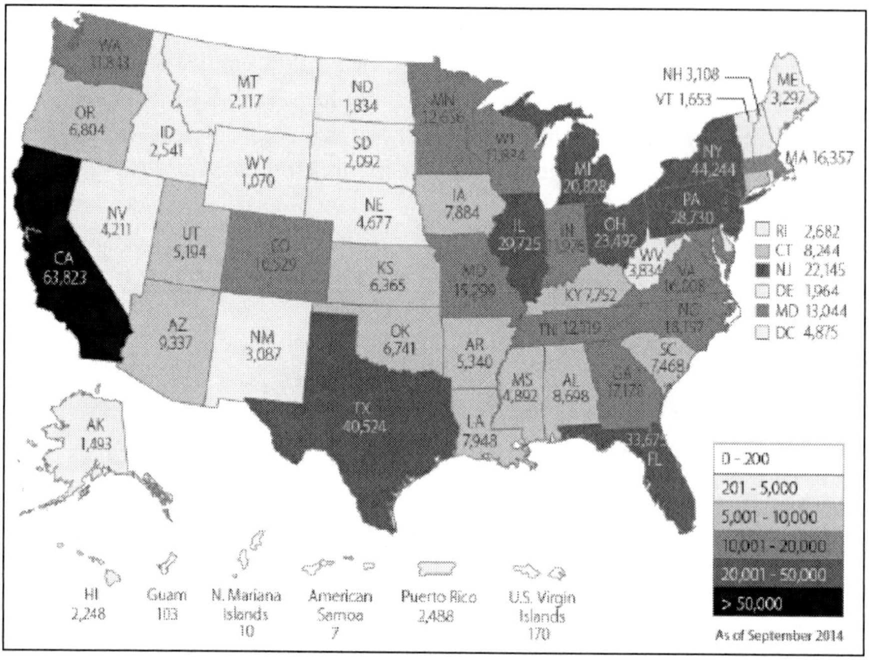

Source: Data provided by USPS staff on June 8, 2015.

Figure 2. U.S. Postal Service Workforce by State.

Figure 3 shows trends in career and non-career USPS employment from FY1995 to FY2014. The number of career employees decreased 35.2% between FY1995 and FY2014, from 753,384 to 488,300. The number of non-career employees, in contrast, increased 6.6% over that time period, from 121,588 to 129,577 (*Table 2).*

Table 1 illustrates career and non-career employees as a percentage of the USPS workforce over the past 20 years. Career employees have constituted the vast majority of USPS's workforce during the past two decades. The proportion of non-career employees, however, has risen since FY1995. The percentage of USPS's workforce that is non-career increased from 13.9% in FY1995 to 21.0% in FY2014. In contrast, the percentage of USPS's workforce consisting of career employees declined from 86.1% to 79.0% between FY1995 and FY2014. (*Figure 4, Table 1*).

FY1995-FY2014

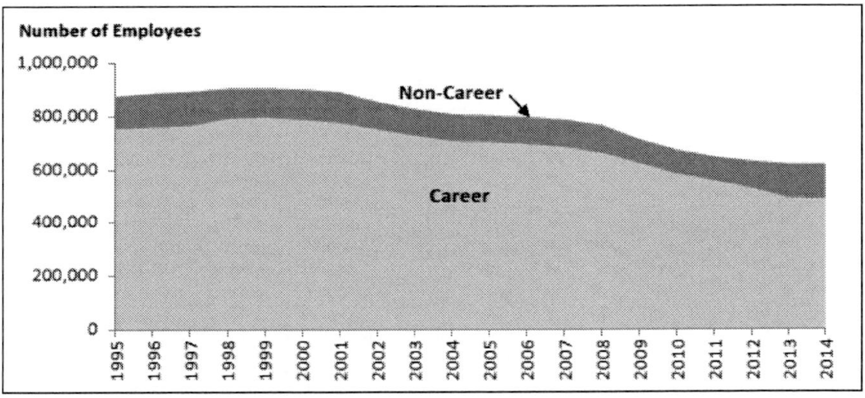

Source: CRS analysis of USPS annual "Form 10-Ks" and USPS "Annual Reports to Congress."

Figure 3. Total Number of Career and Non-Career Employees.

Table 1. Career and Non-Career Employees as a Percentage of the USPS Workforce

FY1995-FY2014 (five-year intervals)

Employees	FY1995	FY2000	FY2005	FY2010	FY2014
Career Employees	86.1%	87.4%	87.8%	86.9%	79.0%
Non-Career Employees	13.9%	12.6%	12.2%	13.1%	21.0%
Total	100.00%	100.00%	100.00%	100.00%	100.00%

Source: CRS analysis of USPS annual "Form 10-Ks" and USPS "Annual Reports to Congress."

Figure 4 shows the yearly percentage change in USPS workforce size, disaggregated by career and non-career employees. As the trend lines indicate, the percentage change in career employees has remained relatively stable, though it has been negative for the past decade. In contrast, the percentage change in non-career employees shows greater variance over time. There was a discernible uptick in the non-career workforce between FY2011 and FY2013—the percentage change in non-career employees increased from a 1.0% gain between FY2010 and FY2011, to a 42.8% gain between FY2011 and FY2013.

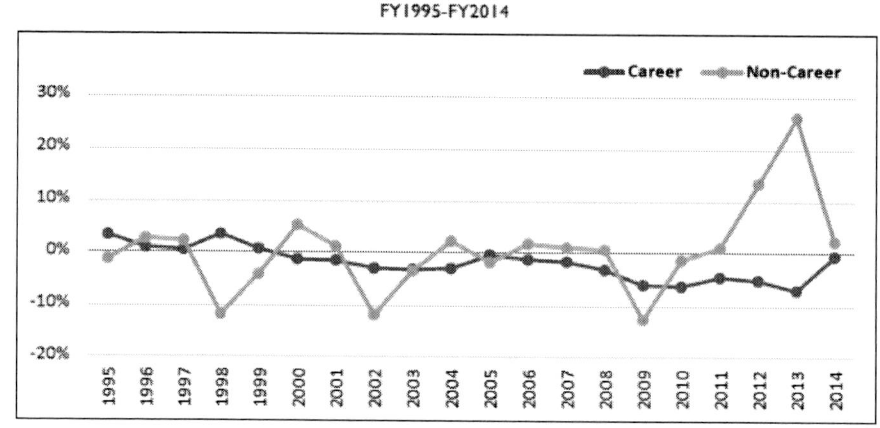

Source: CRS analysis of USPS annual "Form 10-Ks" and USPS "Annual Reports to Congress."

Figure 4. Percentage Change in Career and Non-Career Employees.

Changes in Career Employee Categories

USPS reported data in 19 total career categories since FY1995, though this number includes some categories in which the position had yet to be instituted in FY1995 (N/A in the last column of *Table 2*) or discontinued by FY2014 (−100.00% in the last column of *Table 2*).[6]

Thirteen career employment categories have remained intact between FY1995 and FY2014. Of these categories, 10 had fewer employees in FY2014 than in FY1995.[7] The "Professional Administrative and Technical Personnel" category experienced the greatest percentage decrease in employees from FY1995 to FY2014, with a 60.4% decrease (6,634 fewer employees). Three of the 13 categories of employees populated from FY1995 through FY2014 experienced an increase in their level of employment.[8] "Headquarters" experienced the largest increase in percentage change (60.8%), while "Rural

Delivery Carriers—Full-Time" experienced the largest increase in actual numbers (20,260 more employees).

USPS stated the increase in the number of headquarters employees is primarily attributable to the agency's efforts to centralize certain local, district, and area functions at the headquarters level.[9] Such efforts shifted positions from non-headquarters to headquarters-related categories. For example, USPS centralized human resources (HR) functions at an HR Shared Services Center, which prompted the agency to reallocate positions from field offices to headquarters.[10] While the percentage change in the "Headquarters" category has increased over the past 20 years, the increase is primarily attributable to a significant uptick in employees between FY2003 and FY2004 (41% increase). Since FY2004, the percentage increase in headquarters employees has slowed to 8.3%. In addition, the remaining headquarters-related employment categories that were in place in FY1995 have since decreased.[11]

Changes in Non-Career Employee Categories

USPS has reported data in eight non-career categories since FY1995, which includes categories that were established or eliminated after FY1995.[12] Decreases occurred in three of the four non-career employee categories that have remained intact since FY1995. The number of casuals, or temporary employees who do not receive full-time employee benefits, dropped 93.7% from 26,401 employees in FY1995 to 1,658 in FY2014. The number of "Non-Bargaining Temporary" employees decreased approximately 53.7% from 596 in FY1995 to 276 in FY2014. The number of "Rural Subs/RCA/RCR/AUX" employees decreased 4.3% from 50,269 in FY1995 to 48,099 in FY2014. One non-career category, "PM Relieve/Leave Replacements," experienced an increase of 433 employees (3.4%) from FY1995 to FY2014.

Since FY2011, USPS has established three new non-career employee categories: Postal Support Employees (PSEs), City Carrier Assistants (CCAs), and Mail Handler Assistants (MHAs). As of September 30, 2014, USPS had 24,781 PSEs, 36,081 CCAs, and 5,475 MHAs.[13] PSEs, CCAs, and MHAs were created pursuant to USPS's contract agreement with, respectively, the American Postal Workers Union (APWU), National Association of Letter Carriers (NALC), and National Postal Mail Handlers Union (NPMHU).[14]

The three positions are part of their unions' bargaining units and are eligible for raises, health benefits, and leave.[15]

Table 2. Number of USPS Employees by Employment Category

FY1995-FY2014 (five-year intervals)

Employment Category	FY1995	FY2000	FY2005	FY2010	FY2014	Change FY1995-FY2014	Change (%) FY1995-FY2014
		Career Employees					
Headquarters	1,825	2,279	2,654	2,937	2,934	1,109	60.8%
Headquarters—Related	4,186	5,566	4,333	4,876	3,618	-568	-13.6%
Field Units							
Inspection Service—Field	4,298	4,190	3,443	2,435	2,376	-1,922	-44.7%
Inspector General	0	664	843	1,108	1,132	1,132	N/A
Area Offices Personnel	1,235	1,597	1,420	1,079	818	-417	-33.8%
Postmasters/ Installation	26,564	26,121	25,322	23,111	16,538	-10,026	-37.7%
Heads							
Supervisors/Managers	34,732	38,797	33,234	27,792	23,035	-11,697	-33.7%
Professional Administration and Technical Personnel	10,987	9,959	8,945	5,926	4,353	-6,634	-60.4%
Clerks	273,526	281,956	221,644	0	0	-273,526	-100.0%
Clerks/Nurses	0	0	0	157,168	118,925	118,925	N/A
Nurses	188	191	167	0	0	-188	-100.0%
Mail Handlers	57,352	60,851	56,028	48,650	38,910	-18,442	-32.2%
City Delivery Carriers	239,877	241,079	228,278	192,180	164,626	-72,251	-31.4%
Motor Vehicle Operators	8,029	9,347	8,689	7,413	6,603	-1,426	-17.8%
Rural Delivery Carriers—	46,113	57,111	64,335	66,845	66,373	20,260	43.9%
Full-Time							
Special Delivery Messengers	1,517	0	0	0	0	-1,517	-100.0%
Bldg. and Equip. Maint.	38,161	42,284	39,893	37,403	32,807	-5,354	-14.0%
Personnel							
Vehicle Maintenance	4,794	5,546	5,488	4,985	5,252	458	9.6%
Personnel							
Subtotal	753,384	787,538	704,716	583,908	488,300	-265,084	-35.2%
		Non-Career Employees					
Casuals	26,401	29,572	19,182	6,503	1,658	-24,743	-93.7%
Postal Support Employees	0	0	0	0	24,781	24,781	N/A
Non-bargaining Temporary	596	712	1,185	1,910	276	-320	-53.7%
Rural Subs/RCA/RCR/ AUX	50,269	57,532	57,411	51,801	48,099	-2,170	-4.3%
Postmaster Relief/Leave	12,774	12,423	12,046	11,350	13,207	433	3.4%
Replacements							
City Carrier Assistant	0	0	0	0	36,081	36,081	N/A

Employment Category	FY1995	FY2000	FY2005	FY2010	FY2014	Change FY1995-FY2014	Change (%) FY1995-FY2014
Mail Handler Assistant	0	0	0	0	5,475	5,475	N/A
Transitional Employees	31,548	13,461	8,460	16,215	0	-31,548	-100.0%
Subtotal	121,588	113,700	98,284	87,779	129,577	7,989	6.6%
Total Employees	874,972	901,238	803,000	671,687	617,877	-257,095	-29.4%

Source: CRS analysis of data in USPS "Form 10-Ks" and USPS "Annual Reports to Congress."

Note: In FY2009, USPS reported no nurses in that employment category. In FY2010, "nurses" was joined with "clerks," creating a single employment category. It is unclear why USPS merged those two employment categories, but both "nurses" and "clerks" are represented by the same postal labor union.

Overarching Employment Trends

Although the size of each employment category has shifted over the past 20 years, three overarching trends are apparent. First, the category of full-time rural delivery carriers exhibited moderate growth, rising 43.9% from 46,113 in FY1995 to 66,373 in FY2014. In contrast, the number of city delivery carriers dropped 31.4% from 239,877 in FY1995 to 164,626 in FY2014. USPS has indicated that 65% of population growth occurred in rural areas for much of the 20- year period.[16] USPS further indicated that USPS mail volume increased in these areas through 2009, leading to a greater need for delivery carriers in those areas.[17]

Second, two categories of USPS employees involved in the transportation of mail prior to its delivery grew in the 1990s, peaked around FY2000, and declined below their FY1995 levels in FY2014. The number of mail handlers was 57,352 in FY1995, 62,247 in FY1998, and 38,910 in FY2014. Motor vehicle operators numbered 8,029 in FY1995, 9,347 in FY2000, and 6,603 in FY2014. These downward trends might be due to a decline in mail volume, as well as increased automation of mail transportation functions, over the 20-year period.

Third, the number of non-bargaining temporary employees increased by 493.5% from 596 in FY1995 to 3,537 in FY2012, but has since dropped to 276 in FY2014.

Efforts to Reduce the Size and Cost of the Workforce Between FY2007 and FY2014

In recent years, the USPS has experienced significant financial challenges. After running modest profits from FY2004 through FY2006, the USPS lost $51 billion between FY2007 and FY2014.[18] As USPS's finances have deteriorated, its ability to absorb operating losses has diminished. Between FY2005 and FY2014, USPS's debt rose from $0 to $15 billion.[19] The Government Accountability Office (GAO) added the USPS's financial condition "to the list of high-risk areas needing attention by the Congress and the executive branch."[20] Among the causes for the USPS's financial downturn is the large drop in mail volume in that stretch of time. Between FY2007 and FY2014, the number of mail pieces delivered per year fell from 212 billion to 155 billion.[21] As a result, operating revenues were $7 billion lower in FY2014 ($67.8 billion) than in FY2007 ($74.8 billion).[22]

The USPS's challenging financial circumstances have prompted it to undertake cost-cutting measures. One strategy has been to reduce the size and cost of the USPS workforce, as personnel costs comprise the majority of USPS's expenses. In FY2014, for example, personnel costs represented 78% of USPS's total operating expenses.[23] Two initiatives that USPS pursued between FY2007 and FY2014 to reduce workforce size and cost included (1) attrition and separation incentives, and (2) increased utilization of non-career employees.

Attrition and Separation Incentives

USPS has reduced its workforce size through voluntary attrition and separation incentives to retire or resign.[24] Between FY2007 and FY2014, there was a reduction of 168,052 employees from USPS's workforce.[25] To increase the voluntary attrition rate, USPS has offered certain employees separation incentives to resign or retire early. Those incentives have ranged from $10,000 to $20,000 per person.[26] Between FY2010 and FY2014, 55,473 employees accepted a separation incentive (*Table 3*).

USPS has utilized separation incentives to avoid reductions in force (RIFs), which involve involuntary employee layoffs upon the abolishment of agency positions.[27] On January 9, 2015, however, USPS implemented a reduction in force for 249 postmasters who did not accept a separation incentive offered in

FY2014.[28] Of the 249 postmasters subject to the reduction in force, 169 opted for a Discontinued Service Retirement (DSR), and the remaining 80 who were not eligible for DSR received severance pay based on their age and years of service.[29] According to USPS, all postmasters affected by the RIF were offered part-time career positions at USPS.[30]

Table 3. Total Number of Separated USPS Career Employees

FY2007 – FY2014

Fiscal year	Total number of separations	Total number of employees separated *without* an incentive	Total number of employees separated *with* an incentive	Incentive amount (per person)	Target employee category (incentive)	Total cost of incentive (millions)
2007	7,437	7,437	0	0	N/A	0
2008	33,685	33,685	0	0	N/A	0
2009	42,235	42,235	0	0	N/A	0
2010	40,873	20,073	20,800	$15,000	APWU employees; mailhandlers	$312.0
2011	30,302	28,058	2,244	$20,000	Administra-tive employees	$44.9
2012	33,137	25,920	4,192	$20,000	Postmasters	$129.2
			3,025	$15,000	Mailhandlers	
2013	41,823	17,991	22,609	$15,000	APWU employees	$339.1
			1,223	0	Managers, supervisors, postmasters	
2014	28,900	27,520	1,380	$10,000	Postmasters	$13.8
Total	258,392	202,919	55,473	N/A	N/A	$839.0

Source: Adapted from Table 1 found at GAO, U.S. Postal Service, Status of Workforce Reductions and Related Planning Efforts, GAO-15-43, November 13, 2014, p. 12, at http://www.gao.gov/assets/670/666884.pdf; CRS analysis of data from "Form 10-Ks"; Data provided by USPS staff on June 8, 2015.

Notes: FY2007 data may be incomplete, as USPS only had partial access to data due to a migration from the agency's legacy HR system to its current system during that year. The total number of separated employees is not equal to the total reduction in the number of employees between FY2007 and FY2014. The difference might be due to additional hiring for existing or newly created positions that occurred over that time period.

It is unclear if USPS will continue to use separation incentives to reduce the size of its career workforce. USPS's 2012-2017 business plan, which was updated in April 2013, included a goal to reduce its career workforce to approximately 404,000 employees through attrition by 2017. [31] This represents a 17.3% decrease (84,300 fewer employees) from FY2014 staffing levels. In October 2015, USPS staff stated that the agency was developing an updated five-year business plan. It is possible that the updated plan might contain new strategies for increasing the cost efficiency of the workforce, including the alteration or removal of workforce reduction goals.[32] The use of separation incentives, therefore, might be affected by such altered goals.

Increased Use of Non-Career Employees

USPS has also increased its use of non-career employees in an effort to contain costs. The number of non-career employees increased by 28.1% between FY2007 and FY2014, from 101,167 to 129,577. The number of career employees, in contrast, decreased by 28.7% over the same time period, from 684,762 to 488,300. The most substantial increases occurred between FY2011 and FY2014, during which time the number of non-career employees rose by 46.1% (40,878 more employees). The influx of non-career employees during that time period was primarily attributable to the creation and staffing of PSEs (FY2011), CCAs (FY2013), and MHAs (FY2013).[33] These three employee categories constituted 51% of the USPS non-career workforce in FY2014.[34]

According to USPS and the USPS Office of the Inspector General (OIG), PSEs, CCAs, and MHAs were created to reduce the costs of, and provide more flexibility in, certain agency functions.[35] Employees in these three positions can often perform the full range of duties undertaken by their career counterparts, but at lower wages. For instance, CCAs can perform the duties of career city letter carriers at a starting rate of $15.00 versus $16.71 per hour.[36] The wage difference between CCAs and city letter carriers is even greater after accounting for benefits and overtime ($19.35 versus $46.11 per hour, respectively), according to a 2014 GAO report. USPS asserted that CCAs reduced the cost of the city mail delivery function by $120 million in FY2013.[37] In addition, the USPS OIG reported that PSEs could be used in place of career employees earning overtime, and thus could reduce compensation costs.[38]

USPS's use of certain non-career employees is governed by postal labor union contracts, which limit the number of non-career employees that can comprise the total USPS workforce. More recent labor contracts that created PSEs, CCAs, and MHAs, however, raised the number of non-career employees that can be used for certain functions (*Table 4*). For example, the 2006-2011 contract between USPS and the National Association of Letter Carriers (NALC) limited the total number of non-career transitional employees to no more than 3.5% of the total number of career city letter carriers covered by the agreement or 6% of the total number of career carriers in a postal district.[39] The 2011-2016 contract, however, raised the limit to 15% of the total number of career carriers in a district.[40]

Impact of USPS Initiatives to Reduce Workforce Size and Cost

USPS's initiatives to reduce the size and cost of its workforce have contributed to lowered *compensation expenses* in recent years. USPS's total compensation costs decreased $526 million from FY2013 to FY2014. A 2015 Postal Regulatory Commission (PRC) report found that 36.1% of that amount ($190 million) resulted from increased use of non-career employees and a decrease in employee work hours.[41] The remaining 63.9% of the reduced amount ($336 million) reflected a one-time cost of separation incentives that were paid in FY2013, according the PRC report.[42]

A 2014 GAO report on the USPS workforce, however, found that USPS's *overall* expenses did not decline alongside reduced workforce size and employee work hours.[43] Rather, the report found that USPS's total expenses fluctuated between FY2006 and FY2014.[44] The report attributed the fluctuation to required annual Retiree Health Benefits Fund (RHBF) payments, which varied by year.[45] USPS's overall expenses still declined at a slower rate compared to employee work hours (7.1% versus 24%, respectively) when excluding RHBF payments, according to the report. In response to the GAO report, USPS attributed the slower rate of decline in overall expenses to increased hourly wage and benefit costs, increased non-personnel expenses, and other fixed costs that do not decline with decreases in mail volume.[46]

USPS's 2012-2017 business plan includes several legislative proposals that could affect the size and cost of the workforce.[47] However, USPS staff have indicated that these legislative proposals are no longer being pursued. The agency is focusing on consensus building among stakeholders rather than pursuing a specific legislative agenda.[48]

Table 4. Limitations on the Number of Selected Non-Career Employees

Labor Union	Affected Non-Career Employee Positions	Past Cap	Current Cap
American Postal Workers Union (APWU)	Casuals (past cap) Postal Service Employees (current cap)	6% of the total number of career employees covered by the contract per district[a]	20% of career employees in the clerk craft per district[b]
National Postal Mail Handlers Union (NPHMU)	Casuals (past cap) Mail Handler Assistants (current cap)	12.5% of the total number of employees covered by the contract per installation	15% of career mail handlers per district 20% of career mail handlers per installation 5% of the total number of career employees covered by the contract per installation (casuals)
National Association of Letter Carriers (NALC)	Transitional employees (past cap) City Carrier Assistants (current cap)	3.5% of the total number of city carriers covered by the contract 6% of the total number of career city letter carriers per district	15% of career city letter carriers per district

Source: CRS analysis of contracts between USPS and the APWU, NPHMU, and NALC; information provided by the Postal Regulatory Commission on August 14, 2015, and August 26, 2015.

Notes: Limitations listed under "Current Cap" are stipulated by postal union contracts current through FY2015 and FY2016. Limitations listed under "Past Cap" were stipulated by postal union contracts that expired in FY2010 or FY2011. A postal "district" refers to a zip code area, and a postal "installation" refers to a post office. In contracts that expired in FY2010 or FY2011, non-career employees were referred to as "casuals" or "transitional employees." These positions have been largely replaced by Postal Service Employees (PSEs), City Carrier Assistants (CCAs) and Mail Handler Assistants (MHAs), though some casuals still exist.

[a] As described in the 2006-2010 APWU contract, within the 6% limitation, non-career casuals could not exceed 11% of career clerk craft employees at installations with 200 or more workyears of employment in the regular workforce.

[b] The 2010-2015 APWU contract places additional limits on retail (window) clerks. In larger offices (Level 22 and above), PSEs working retail windows cannot exceed

10% of the career retail clerks in the installation. In smaller offices (Level 21 and below), PSEs cannot exceed 20% of the career retail clerks.

[c] In addition, the 2006-2011 NALC contract requires installations with 200 or more workyears of employment in the regular workforce to be 88% staffed by career letter carriers.

[d] The 2011-2016 NALC contract allowed USPS to exceed the 15% limitation and hire an additional 8,000 CCAs to provide new products and services. The number of additional CCAs, however, cannot exceed 8% of the total number of career city delivery carriers in the district for any one reporting period.

Appendix. Brief Descriptions of USPS Employment Categories[49]

Career Employees

Area Offices Personnel: Includes persons who work in the USPS administrative units that oversee postal operations in USPS's nine geographic areas throughout the United States.

Building and Equipment Maintenance Personnel: Includes persons who maintain and repair USPS facilities.

Clerks: Includes persons who work directly with the public in USPS retail facilities and who manually sort mail.

City Delivery Carriers: Includes persons who deliver mail in urban and non-rural areas.

Headquarters: Includes persons who work in a variety of capacities at the two central offices of the U.S. Postal Service, which are located in Washington, DC, and Rosslyn, VA.

Headquarters—Related Field Units: Includes persons in offices administered from USPS's headquarters, but who are located elsewhere.

Inspection Service—Field: Includes persons who work for the Postal Inspection Service, which protects USPS property and employees and investigates alleged misuse of the mails for criminal purposes.

Inspector General: Includes persons who work for the USPS Office of Inspector General, which audits and investigates USPS activities.

Mail Handlers: Includes persons who move mail containers in mail processing centers. **Motor Vehicle Operators:** Includes persons who drive mail trucks.

Nurses: Includes persons who work in USPS medical units and attend to injured employees.

Postmasters/Installation Heads: Includes persons who serve as managers of retail postal facilities.

Professional Administrative and Technical Personnel: Includes persons performing administrative assistance and technical support duties.

Regional Offices: Included persons in the administrative unit that oversaw USPS operations within geographic regions. Regional offices were replaced with area offices.

Rural Delivery Carriers—Full-time: Includes persons who deliver mail in non-urban areas.

Special Delivery Messengers: Discontinued position that employed persons to make deliveries that required expedited delivery.

Supervisors/Managers: Includes persons who supervise other persons or who manage programs or processes.

Vehicle Maintenance Personnel: Includes persons who perform preventive maintenance and repair of USPS vehicles.

Non-Career Employees

Casuals: Includes persons hired temporarily to assist USPS career employees in mail processing facilities.

City Carrier Assistant: Time-limited position created in 2013 that provides the USPS with flexibility in hiring for the city delivery function. City Carrier Assistants may perform the full range of duties undertaken by career City Delivery Carriers and are entitled to certain employee benefits such as raises, health benefits, and leave.[50]

Mail Handler Assistant: Time-limited position created in 2013 that provides the USPS with flexibility in hiring for the mail delivery function. Mail Handler Assistants may perform the full range of duties undertaken by career Mail Handlers and are entitled to certain employee benefits such as raises, health benefits, and leave.[51]

Non-bargaining Temporary: Includes persons hired temporarily to perform administrative duties in USPS offices.

Postal Support Employees: Time-limited position created in 2011 that provides the USPS with flexibility in hiring within the clerk craft and the maintenance and motor vehicle craft. Pursuant to a bargaining agreement,

Postal Support Employees are entitled to certain employees benefits such as raises, health benefits, and leave.[52]

Postmaster Relief/Leave Replacements: Includes persons who serve temporarily as managers of retail postal facilities.

Rural Subs/RCA/RCR/AUX: Includes rural substitute carriers, rural carrier associates, rural carrier relief carriers, and auxiliary carriers, all of whom provide temporary assistance to USPS in the delivery of mail in non-urban areas.

Transitional Employees: Includes persons who staff USPS's Remote Encoding Centers (RECs), which provide assistance concerning mail processing machines.[53]

End Notes

[1] Workforce data was obtained from the following sources: U.S. Postal Service (hereafter USPS), Annual Report of the Postmaster General (Washington: USPS, 1985-1995); USPS, Annual Report of the United States Postal Service (Washington: USPS, 1996-2010); and USPS, Report on Form 10-K (Washington: USPS, 2007-2014).

[2] For more information on the Great Recession, see CRS Report R40198, The 2007-2009 Recession: Similarities to and Differences from the Past, by Marc Labonte.

[3] The employee categories that comprise both career and non-career employee types are defined in the Appendix. Non-career employees do not include persons carrying out postal-related functions outsourced to private firms. For example, USPS no longer has a fleet of cargo aircraft. Today, USPS contracts with private firms for the transportation of mail by air. The persons who fly and maintain these planes are not included in the data on non-career employees.

[4] For a list of benefits provided to USPS career employees, see USPS, "Compensation and Benefits," at https://about.usps.com/careers/working-usps/benefits.htm.

[5] USPS, Employee and Labor Relations Manual, ELM 36, September 2013, p. 572, at http://about.usps.com/manuals/elm/elmc5.pdf.

[6] Since FY1995, USPS has added an Office of Inspector General, which, at the end of FY2014, had 1,132 employees. In FY2009, USPS had no "nurses" in the "nurses" category. In FY2010, USPS merged the "clerks" and "nurses" categories. As of FY1999, USPS discontinued the "Special Delivery Messengers" category. USPS reported data for "Discontinued Operations" in FY1996, but did not report employees in this category for any other succeeding year.

[7] These categories include Headquarters—Related Field Units (prior to FY2012, Headquarters—Field Support Units), Inspection Service—Field, Area Offices, Postmasters/Installation Heads, Supervisors/Managers, Professional Administrative and Technical Personnel, Mail Handlers, City Delivery Carriers, Motor Vehicle Operators, and Building and Equipment Maintenance Personnel.

[8] These categories include Headquarters, Rural Delivery Carriers—Full-Time, and Vehicle Maintenance Personnel.

[9] Information provided electronically by USPS staff on September 26, 2014.

[10] Ibid. The changes to specific employment categories affected by this consolidation, as well as the extent to which new hires were used to fill these new positions, are not clear.

[11] CRS analysis of USPS "Form 10-Ks" and USPS "Annual Reports to Congress." These categories include: Headquarters – Field Support Units and Inspection Service – Field.

[12] In FY2011, USPS added the "Postal Support Employees" category. In FY2013, USPS discontinued the "Transitional Employees" category and added the "City Carrier Assistant" and "Mail Handler Assistant" categories.

[13] Pursuant to the American Postal Workers Union contract, employees categorized as "casuals" were to be converted to the PSE category where appropriate. See American Postal Workers Union (hereafter APWU), Collective Bargaining Agreement Between APWU and USPS, November 21, 2010-May 20, 2015, p. 308, at http://www.apwu.org/sites/apwu/files/resource-files/APWU%20Contract%202010-2015.pdf.

[14] Ibid. pp. 19-22 and 279-296; National Association of Letter Carriers (hereafter NALC) and USPS, 2011-2016 National Agreement Between NALC and USPS, pp. 16-18, at http://www.nalc.org/member-benefits/body/na2011.pdf; National Postal Mail Handlers Union (hereafter NPMHU) and USPS, Agreement Between NPMHU and USPS, November 21, 2011-May 20, 2016, pp. 13-14 and 125-133, at http://www.npmhu.org/resources/document/ USPSNPMHU2011NationalAgreement.pdf.

[15] Ibid. For more information on USPS's financial condition, see CRS Report R43162, The U.S. Postal Service's Financial Condition: A Primer, by Daniel J. Richardson.

[16] Information provided electronically from USPS on September 24, 2014.

[17] Ibid.

[18] CRS analysis of USPS "Form 10-Ks."

[19] Ibid.

[20] U.S. Government Accountability Office (hereafter GAO), Restructuring the U.S. Postal Service to Achieve Sustainable Financial Viability, GAO-09-937SP, July 28, 2009, p. 1, at http://www.gao.gov/assets/210/203772.pdf.

[21] USPS, 2007 Report on Form 10-K, p. 11, at http://about.usps.com/who-we-are/financials/10k-reports/fy2007.pdf; USPS, 2014 Report on Form 10-K, pp. 16.

[22] USPS, 2014 Report on Form 10-K, p. 13; USPS, 2008 Report on the Form 10-K, p. 12, November 25, 2008, at http://about.usps.com/who-we-are/financials/10k-reports/fy2008.pdf. For more information on USPS's financial condition, see CRS Report R43162, The U.S. Postal Service's Financial Condition: A Primer, by Daniel J. Richardson.

[23] Information provided by USPS to CRS on January 21, 2015.

[24] USPS, 2014 Report on the Form 10-K, December 5, 2014, p. 20.

[25] CRS analysis of data provided by USPS.

[26] USPS has utilized the Voluntary Early Retirement Authority (VERA) and Voluntary Separation Incentive Program (VSIP). For more information on the VERA, see 5 U.S.C. §8336(d)(2)(D), 5 U.S.C. §8414(b)(1)(B), 5 C.F.R. §831.114, 5 C.F.R. §842.213, and OPM, Guide To Voluntary Early Retirement Regulations, August 2006, at https://www.opm.gov/policy-data-oversight/workforce-restructuring/voluntary-early-retirement-authority/ vera_guide.pdf. For more information on the VSIP, see 5 U.S.C. §3521, 5 C.F.R. part 576, and OPM, Guide to Voluntary Separation Incentive Payments, August 2006, at https://www.opm.gov/policy-data-oversight/workforcerestructuring/voluntary-separation-incentive-payments/guide.pdf.

[27] For more information on reductions in force, see 5 U.S.C. §3501-3503, and 5 C.F.R. Part 351.

[28] Electronic correspondence with USPS staff on June 8, 2015.

[29] For more information on Discontinued Service Retirement, see 5 U.S.C. §8336(d) and 5 C.F.R. §831.503.

[30] Ibid.

[31] USPS, Five Year Business Plan, April 2013, p. 28, at http://about.usps.com/strategic-planning/fiveyearplan04162013-final.pdf. USPS anticipated a reduction of approximately 146,000 career and non-career full-time equivalents by 2017.

[32] Electronic correspondence with USPS staff on October 8, 2015.

[33] CRS analysis of annual USPS "Form 10-Ks."

[34] CRS analysis of USPS "Form 10-Ks."

[35] USPS Office of the Inspector General, Use of Non-Traditional Full-Time and Postal Support Employee Positions in Processing Operations, May 17, 2013, p. 1, at https://www.uspsoig.gov/sites/default/files/document-library-files/2013/ no-ar-13-003.pdf; U.S. Postal Service, 2013 Report on Form 10-K, p. 31; National Postal Mail Handlers Union, AFL-CIO, and U.S. Postal Service, Board of Interest Arbitration Award, August 5, 2014, p. 12-13; and information provided electronically to CRS from USPS on August 15, 2014.

[36] NALC and USPS, 2011-2016 National Agreement, p. 28, at http://www.nalc.org/member-benefits/body/na2011.pdf; GAO, U.S. Postal Service, Status of Workforce Reductions and Related Planning Efforts, GAO-15-43, November 13 2014, p. 18, at http://www.gao.gov/assets/670/666884.pdf.

[37] USPS, 2013 Report on Form 10-K, p. 31.

[38] USPS OIG, Use of Non-Traditional Full-Time and Postal Support Employee Positions in Processing Operations, Report Number NO-AR-13-003, May 17, 2013, p. 5, at https://www.uspsoig.gov/sites/default/files/document-libraryfiles/2013/no-ar-13-003.pdf.

[39] NALC and USPS, 2006-2011 National Agreement, p. 15, at http://www.nalc.org/workplace-issues/contractadministration-unit/body/na2006.pdf. The 2006 agreement places limitations on the number of "transitional employees," a non-career employee category that was phased out and replaced by CCAs in 2013.

[40] NALC and USPS, 2011-2016 National Agreement, p. 16.

[41] USPS, 2014 Report on the Form 10-K, December 5, 2014, p. 20; PRC, Financial Analysis of United States Postal Service Financial Results and 10-K Statement, Fiscal Year 2014, April 1, 2015, p. 12. Total compensation does not include retirement, health benefits, workers' compensation, or Retiree Health Benefits Fund (RHBF) payments.

[42] Postal Regulatory Commission, Financial Analysis of United States Postal Service Financial Results and 10-K Statement, Fiscal Year 2014, April 1, 2015, p. 12.

[43] Government Accountability Office, U.S. Postal Service, Status of Workforce Reductions and Related Planning Efforts, GAO-15-43, November 13, 2014. The report analyzed several initiatives to reduce the size and cost of the USPS workforce, including separation incentives, use of non-career employees, and other initiatives to consolidate and streamline operations that impact workforce size and cost.

[44] Ibid., pp. 9-10.

[45] Ibid., pp. 10-11.

[46] Ibid., p. 11.

[47] USPS, Five Year Business Plan, April 16, 2013, p. 26. A more detailed description of each legislative goal can be found at USPS, http://about.usps.com/news/testimony/2013/pr13_pmg0213.htm.

[48] Information provided by USPS staff on September 17, 2015.

[49] Unless otherwise noted, these employment categories are those used by USPS in its Annual Report and were composed by the author of this report in consultation with USPS.

[50] The definition for City Carrier Assistant was created by CRS using National Association of Letter Carriers, "Key Provisions of the 2011-2016 National Agreement Arbitration Award."

[51] The definition for Mail Handler Assistant was created by CRS using National Postal Mail Handlers Union, "Questions and Answers 2011-2016 Fishgold Arbitration Award."

[52] The definition for Postal Support Employees was created by CRS using U.S. Postal Service, "Postal Service Establishes New Position," Press Release, June 8, 2011, at http://about.usps.com/news/state-releases/fl/2011/ fl_2011_0610.htm.

[53] If a mail processing machine cannot read an address, it makes an electronic image of the mail piece and transmits the image to a computer at an REC. There an employee attempts to determine the correct address for the mail piece so that it may be reentered into the mail processing stream.

In: U.S. Postal Service Reform
Editor: Martin Thomas

ISBN: 978-1-53610-463-9

Chapter 3

U.S. POSTAL SERVICE RETIREE HEALTH BENEFITS AND PENSION FUNDING ISSUES*

Kevin R. Kosar and Katelin P. Isaacs

SUMMARY

Congress designed the U.S. Postal Service (USPS) to be a self-supporting government agency. Since 1971, the agency has not relied upon annual appropriations to cover its operating costs. Rather, USPS has funded its operations mostly through the sales of postage and postal products and services.

Since FY2007, however, the agency has run more than $40 billion in deficits and has reached its statutory borrowing limit ($15 billion). The agency does receive an annual appropriation of approximately $90 million per year, which amounts to about 0.1% of USPS's $65 billion operating budget.

USPS's troubled financial condition has raised concerns about the viability of the agency. Many postal reform bills have been introduced in the 113th and 112th Congresses. These bills have proposed altering many aspects of postal operations, from raising the rates mailers pay to reducing the days of delivery and closing USPS post offices and mail sorting facilities.

Postal reform bills also have proposed alterations to the policies for funding the retiree healthcare and pensions for USPS's workforce.

---

* This is an edited, reformatted and augmented version of a Congressional Research Service publication, R43349, dated January 2, 2014.

Alterations to these policies could significantly affect USPS's financial condition. Pre-funding USPS's retiree health benefits cost the agency $5.6 billion in FY2013, and funding its pensions cost $5.7 billion. These retiree healthcare and pension costs constitute 15.7% of the agency's operating expenses.

USPS employees are covered by the same retirement plans as most other civilian federal employees: the Civil Service Retirement System (CSRS) and the Federal Employees' Retirement System (FERS). In addition, USPS retirees (and employees) participate in the Federal Employees Health Benefits Program (FEHBP). Since FY2007, USPS has been required by law to prefund its current employees' future retirement health benefits at a cost of more than $5 billion per year. USPS has lacked sufficient cash to make all of these payments.

A number of bills have been introduced in the 113th Congress to improve USPS's financial condition by altering current pension and retiree health benefits funding policies. Bills carrying provisions to alter the funding of USPS retiree health benefits include H.R. 630, H.R. 2690, H.R. 2748, and S. 1486. Current USPS pension funding legislation includes H.R. 630, H.R. 961, H.R. 2690, H.R. 2748, S. 316, and S. 1486.

The aforementioned USPS retiree health benefits bills would reduce the Postal Service's annual operating expenses by abolishing or reworking the current statutory prefunding schedule; moving some USPS retirees on to Medicare; or lowering the target for prefunding from the current 100% funding requirement to 80% of the estimated total liability.

The USPS pension-related bills aim to aid the Postal Service's financial condition by either changing the allocation of costs between the Postal Service and the federal government in the funding of USPS CSRS benefits or recalculating USPS's FERS costs. In both instances, the legislation would refund sums from the federal government to USPS.

BACKGROUND

In 1971, Congress established the U.S. Postal Service (USPS) and mandated that it operate as a self-supporting, wholly governmental entity.[1]Previously, the federal government provided postal services via the U.S. Post Office Department (USPOD), a federal agency that was financially dependent upon annual appropriations from Congress. Members of Congress were involved in many aspects of the USPOD's operations, including the selection of managers (e.g., postmasters) and the pricing of postal services.

In 1971, Congress enacted the Postal Reorganization Act (PRA; P.L. 91-375), which replaced USPOD with USPS—an "independent establishment of the executive branch."[2] The PRA designed USPS to be a marketized government agency, that is, an agency that would cover its operating costs with revenues generated through the sales of postage and related products and services.[3] Although USPS does receive an annual appropriation, the agency does not rely on appropriations. Its appropriation is approximately $90 million per year, about 0.1% of USPS's $65 billion operating budget.[4] Congress provides this appropriation to compensate USPS for the revenue it forgoes in providing, at congressional direction, free mailing privileges to blind persons and overseas voters. Otherwise, USPS by law is directed to cover the costs of its operations from revenues deposited in the Postal Service Fund, a revolving account at the U.S. Treasury. Thus, USPS's operational costs are to be borne not by the public as a whole, but by ratepayers (i.e., those individuals and organizations who purchase postage).

USPS employees are covered by, and may be eligible for, benefits under the same two pension plans that cover nearly all civilian federal workers: the Civil Service Retirement System (CSRS) for employees first hired before 1984, and the Federal Employees' Retirement System (FERS) for employees first hired in 1984 or later.[5] In addition, by law, USPS retirees (and employees) may participate in the Federal Employees Health Benefits Program (FEHBP).[6]

USPS's recent deficits—$40 billion since FY2007—have prompted much discussion over possible reforms to the agency and its operations.[7] USPS's retiree health benefits and pension funding policies have been part of this discussion, in part because they represent significant costs to the agency. Pre-funding USPS's retiree health benefits cost the agency $5.6 billion in FY2013, and funding its pensions cost $5.7 billion.[8] This amounted to 15.7% of the USPS's $72.1 billion operating expenses.

In addition, there are concerns over the possible negative ramifications on postal retirees and the public were USPS to insufficiently fund its retirees' health benefits or pensions. For example, the Office of Personnel Management (OPM) reports that the U.S. Treasury (and, therefore, taxpayers) would be liable for any USPS shortfalls in funding its pensions.[9]

RECENT USPS RETIREE HEALTH BENEFITS FUNDING ISSUES[10]

Since FY2007, USPS has been required to prefund its current employees' future retirement benefits. This policy was included in an omnibus postal reform law, the Postal Accountability and Enhancement Act (P.L. 109-435, hereinafter "PAEA," enacted in December 2006).[11] This prefunding policy has become contentious since USPS began posting multi-billion dollar financial losses in FY2007 and missing pre-payments.[12]

The debates concerning retiree health benefits prefunding have centered on both the principle of prefunding and the PAEA's execution thereof. Hence, some in Congress have advocated abolishing the prefunding requirement entirely. Others in Congress have proposed various ways to revise the PAEA's funding schedule so as to continue prefunding but to alleviate USPS's costs in the short term.

The PAEA Prefunding Requirement

Prior to the enactment of the PAEA, USPS funded its share of retiree health premiums on a pay-as-you-go basis. Put in simple terms, formerly USPS annually tabulated the number of retirees and then paid its portion of the health premiums due for those retirees. (USPS retirees also pay a portion of their health premiums.)[13]

The PAEA required USPS to continue contributing to current retirees' benefits from the Postal Service Fund each year. The law also obliged USPS annually to set aside funds for the future retiree health benefits of current employees.[14]

Specifically, the PAEA created a 50-year payment schedule,[15] which includes 10 years of statutorily prescribed prefunding payments (FY2007-FY2016) into the Postal Service Retiree Health Benefits Fund (RHBF).[16] *Table 1* depicts the statutorily prescribed prepayments.[17]

In FY2017, the statutorily prescribed payment amounts conclude. Between FY2017 and FY2056, however, USPS would continue to make annual payments to RHBF. The amount of these payments would be determined OPM. Per PAEA, OPM is to compute on an annual basis, the size of current employees' future retiree healthcare benefit liability and the current RHBF balance and then to determine a schedule of annual payments to liquidate any outstanding liability by September 30, 2056.[18]

Disputes over Prefunding Future Retiree Health Benefits

Although enacted with little, if any, ostensible criticism, the PAEA's prefunding policy subsequently has become very contentious.[19]

Table 1. USPS Future Retiree Health Benefits Payment Schedule

Fiscal Year	Payment Due Per PAEA (billions)	Status of Payment
2007	$5.4	Paid in full.
2008	$5.6	Paid in full.
2009	$5.4	$1.4 billion paid.[a]
2010	$5.5	Paid in full.
2011	$5.5	No payment.[b]
2012	$5.6	No payment.
2013	$5.6	No payment.
2014	$5.7	Due September 30, 2014.
2015	$5.7	Due September 30, 2015.
2016	$5.8	Due September 30, 2016.

Source: Postal Accountability and Enhancement Act (P.L. 109-435, §803; 120 Stat. 3251-3252; 5 U.S.C §8909(d)(3)(A)) and USPS Annual Reports.

[a] Congress reduced the FY2009 payment amount from $5.4 billion to $1.4 billion (P.L. 111-68, §164).

[b] Congress delayed the FY2011 payment due date to October 4, 2011 (P.L. 112-33, §124), November 18, 2011 (P.L. 112-36, §124), December 16, 2011 (P.L. 112-55, §101), and then August 1, 2012 (H.Rept. 112- 331, §632).

The criticisms of prefunding include the following:

1. For 36 years (1970-2006), USPS paid its current retiree health benefits out of pocket without incident.
2. No other federal agency prefunds its current employees' future retirement health benefits, so it is unfair to require USPS to do so.[20]
3. Private-sector companies that prefund their future retiree health benefits do not typically fund 100% of the obligation.[21]
4. Prefunding was primarily a policy designed to contend with a budget scoring issue caused by USPS overfunding its pensions.[22]
5. Prefunding is financially harming USPS—it is draining USPS's cash, and it has had a significant role in producing the agency's recent deficits.[23]

Arguments advanced in favor of prefunding include the following:

1. The pay-as-you-go approach creates an inaccurate depiction of USPS's financial health. "Because the Service was ignoring a very

expensive fringe benefit in its income statement, its reported costs were artificially low and its reported income artificially high."[24]
2. The pay-as-you-go approach is inequitable in that "current [postage] ratepayers are not paying for the full costs of the services they are receiving." Instead, a portion of current employees' compensation costs will be paid by future mailers.[25]
3. "Based on known demographic trends, the Service's share of its retirees' health insurance premiums is expected to continue rising until about 2040. Under the Service's existing accounting and rate-setting methods, more significant and frequent rate hikes are likely to be needed for future ratepayers to cover the costs of benefits that are being earned by current employees."[26]
4. The prefunding of future retirement benefits provides compensation security for current employees.[27]
5. Prefunding future retiree health benefits protects U.S. taxpayers from a possible bailout should USPS health benefits costs exceed USPS's cash on hand.[28]

Beyond these debates, two additional issues have arisen with the PAEA prefunding policy as enacted. First USPS has not had sufficient cash to meet the current statutory RHBF payment schedule. Second there have been actuarial disputes over the size of USPS's future retiree health benefits liability and, by implication, over the size of the annual FY2007 to FY2016 RHBF payments required.

USPS's Difficulties in Meeting the RHBF Payment Schedule

While the principle of prefunding continues to be debated, a more recent concern is the practicality of the FY2007 to FY2016 payment schedule. In short, although the law states USPS must pay more than $5.0 billion per year through FY2017, the agency has not had sufficient cash to make all these payments.[29]

Between FY2007 and FY2012, USPS's financial condition eroded considerably. Mail volume fell 25.1%, from 212 billion pieces to 159 billion pieces.[30] USPS's revenue declined 12.8%, from $74.8 billion to $65.2 billion. The agency's debt grew from $4.2 billion (FY2007) to $15 billion, the maximum amount permitted by statute.[31] The fall in revenues combined with the FY2007 and FY2008 RHBF payments have drained the agency's cash supply.

USPS's difficulties in meeting the RHBF payment schedule date from FY2009, when Congress reduced that year's payment owed from $5.4 billion to $1.4 billion. This relief helped USPS have sufficient cash on hand to make the FY2010 payment. Since then, however, the agency has defaulted on the FY2011, FY2012, and FY2013 RHBF payments.[32]

Disputes over the Size of USPS's RHBF Liability and Annual RHBF Payments

In FY2012, OPM calculated USPS's future retiree health benefits liability to be $93.6 billion.[33] OPM estimated USPS had funded $45.7 billion of this obligation, which leaves an unfunded obligation of $47.9 billion.

The estimation of healthcare costs requires making certain assumptions. Thus, USPS has noted,

> [b]ecause calculation of this [retiree health benefit] liability involves several areas of judgment, estimates of the liability could vary significantly depending on the assumptions used. Utilizing the same underlying data that was used in preparing the [above] estimate... the September 30, 2012, unfunded obligation could range from $35 billion to $63 billion, solely by varying the inflation rate by plus or minus 1%, and the 2011 unfunded obligation would range from $34 billion to $60 billion.[34]

The size of USPS's estimated health benefits obligation is consequential; it affects the agency's reported financial results because the Postal Service is expected to pay these obligations that are owed to retirees. The larger the obligation, generally, the larger the yearly USPS outlays that would need to be made to retire that obligation.[35]

Both the U.S. Postal Service Office of Inspector General (USPSOIG) and the Postal Regulatory Commission (PRC) have released studies arguing that the size of USPS's future retirees' health benefits obligation likely will be lower than OPM has estimated.[36] USPSOIG and PRC concluded that USPS could have paid $1.6 billion per year and $3.2 billion per year, respectively, between FY2007 and FY2016 to adequately fund its future retiree healthcare obligation. The differences between these estimates are due to the differing assumptions used. For example, OPM assumed healthcare costs would rise 7% per year, whereas USPSOIG assumed a rate of 5% per year. OPM assumed USPS's workforce size would stay the same size; PRC assumed USPS's employee cohort would become smaller due to downsizing.[37]

Recent Proposals for Changing the Prefunding Policy

In the 113th Congress, bills have been introduced to change the current RHBF policy. These bills either propose to eliminate the RHBF payment schedule or to modify it so as to reduce the size of the annual payments. These bills include[38]

- The Postal Service Protection Act of 2013 (H.R. 630) and (S. 316), which would abolish the RHBF prefunding policy and RHBF payment schedule.[39]
- The Innovate to Deliver Act of 2013 (H.R. 2690), which would replace the current RHBF payment schedule with a new payment schedule. USPS would make no RHBF payments until 2016. The total liability would be amortized between the years of 2016 and 2053. H.R. 2690 also would require USPS to fund 80% of its total liability (as opposed to the current 100% funding requirement).[40]
- The House version of the Postal Reform Act of 2013 (H.R. 2748), which would replace the current RHBF payment schedule with a new payment schedule. USPS would make no RHBF payments until 2016. The total liability would be amortized between the years of 2016 and 2056. H.R. 2748 also would require USPS to fund 80% of its total liability (as opposed to the current 100% funding requirement).[41]
- The Senate version of the Postal Reform Act of 2013 (S. 1486), which would replace the current RHBF payment schedule with a new payment schedule. USPS would make no RHBF payments until 2016. The total liability would be amortized between the years of 2016 and 2052. S. 1486 also would attempt to reduce USPS's long-term retiree health benefits costs by moving some USPS retirees onto Medicare, and by authorizing USPS to opt its employees (and future retirees) out of the Federal Employees Health Benefits Plan and into a new health insurance program.[42] Finally, the bill aims to further reduce USPS's pre-funding costs by requiring USPS to fund 80% of its total liability (as opposed to the current 100% funding requirement).

RECENT USPS PENSION FUNDING ISSUES[43]

Recent policy debate has focused on two issues related to the funding of retirement benefits for USPS employees. First, the allocation of costs between USPS and the federal government in the funding of USPS benefits under CSRS has been debated. Second, the issue of a surplus or "overpayment" made by USPS on behalf of its FERS employees has been identified; although amendments to current law would be required to refund any payments to USPS.

USPS CSRS Funding: Allocation of Costs

CSRS provides pension benefits to eligible USPS employees and other federal employees first hired prior to 1984.[44] When the Postal Reorganization Act (PRA; P.L. 91-375) created USPS in 1971, the law resulted in a situation in which some USPS employees performed service under CSRS as employees of both (1) the old USPOD and (2) the newly created USPS. The required CSRS employer contributions made by USPS on behalf of its CSRS employees are no different than the employer contributions made by other federal agencies; however, it was not immediately clear how the funding of CSRS benefits for employees with service under both USPOD and USPS should be assigned. The PRA did not specifically allocate responsibility for the costs of CSRS benefits for these individuals between USPS and the federal government.

In 1974, P.L. 93-349 required that responsibility for the costs of CSRS retirement benefits due to pay increases granted by USPS (i.e., pay increases after July 1, 1971) be transferred to USPS from the federal government.[45] Subsequently, the Postal Civil Service Retirement System Funding Reform Act of 2003 (P.L. 108-18), made USPS liable for the full dynamic normal cost of all CSRS benefits attributable to post-1971 service.[46] In 2006, PAEA (P.L. 109-435) made additional changes to the methodology used by OPM in determining a USPS funding surplus or liability for CSRS benefits.

Under current law, OPM calculates the pay and benefits accrued for CSRS employees under USPOD separately from the pay and benefits accrued under USPS. The federal government is responsible for the costs of the former service, while USPS is responsible for the costs of the latter service. Therefore, for an employee with 15 years of USPOD service and 15 years of USPS service, his or her CSRS benefit would be financed by the federal government based on the pay and the 15 years of service prior to 1971 and by USPS based on final pay and the 15 years of service beginning in 1971. Because pay generally rises as job tenure increases (and P.L. 93-349 required USPS to finance the retirement costs of any pay increases beginning in 1971), the pay measure used to calculate the federal government's share of the CSRS benefit cost in this example is lower than the pay measure used to calculate USPS's share of the benefit cost. Thus, in this example, USPS would finance a larger portion of the cost of the CSRS benefit than the federal government.

Two agencies with USPS oversight or auditing functions have asserted that OPM's current method of allocation of the costs of CSRS benefits for employees with service under both USPOD and USPS is incorrect. For instance, a January 2010 report issued by USPSOIG claimed that the allocation of CSRS pension costs for employees with service as USPOD and USPS employees should be directly proportional to the number of years spent employed by each agency.[47] That is, in the example of an employee with 15 years of USPOD service and 15 years of USPS service, the federal government should fund one-half of this individual's CSRS annuity and USPS should fund one-half of the retirement benefit.

A June 2010 report issued by PRC maintained that final high-three pay rather than 1971 salary should be used in calculating the federal government's portion of these CSRS benefits.[48] As stated above, pay generally rises as job tenure increases; therefore, this method of calculation would increase the pay measure used to calculate the federal government's liability, thereby shifting the cost of CSRS benefits from USPS to the federal government for individuals with service under both USPOD and USPS. In the example used above of an employee with 15 years of USPOD service and 15 years of USPS service, the federal government would fund the first 15 years of service at a benefit accrual percentage of 26.25% and USPS would fund the next 15 years of service at a 30.00% benefit accrual percentage—both at the same high-three final pay.[49]

According to recent analyses conducted by the Office of Personnel Management Office of Inspector General (OPMOIG), however, neither the Postal Civil Service Retirement System Funding Reform Act of 2003 (P.L. 108-18) nor PAEA changed the fundamental allocation of costs for increased CSRS benefits due to post-1971 salary increases between USPS and the federal government as set out under P.L. 93-349.[50]

In addition, in a December 2011 analysis of this issue, the U.S. Government Accountability Office (GAO) concluded:

> OPM has carried out this requirement [under P.L. 93-349] by calculating the retirement costs for pre-1971 service (those that the federal government is responsible for) based on the employee's credited service and rate of basic pay on June 30, 1971, the last day the [US]POD was in existence. In our view, the 2003 and 2006 Acts did not change the fundamental allocation made by the 1974 Act and thus OPM's current methodology continues to be consistent with law.[51]

Because past laws have set out the current method of allocation—P.L. 93-349; P.L. 108-18; and PAEA—any reallocation of costs for USPS CSRS employees with service under both USPOD and USPS would require changes to law. Absent a reduction in the cost of financing CSRS pensions, a reduction in the proportion of CSRS pension costs allocated to USPS—as under the USPSOIG and PRC reports—would increase the current unfunded liability of the Civil Service Retirement and the Disability Fund (CSRDF), the federal trust fund that finances CSRS and FERS benefits. This reallocation of CSRS costs would also result in an equal increase in CSRS pension expenses borne by the U.S. Treasury.

USPS FERS Funding: Overpayment

FERS covers most of the civilian federal workforce, including USPS employees, first hired in 1984 and later.[52] FERS is required to be fully funded under 5 U.S.C. §8423. By law, the FERS retirement benefit must be prefunded according to its dynamic normal cost. The dynamic normal cost of a pension represents the amount of funds that must be set aside annually to fully fund benefits for workers who will continue to accrue new benefits, including the effects of employee pay raises, post-retirement cost-of-living adjustments (COLAs), and changes in the rate of interest.

Federal agencies and USPS are required to make FERS contributions at a rate that is the dynamic normal cost of FERS minus required employee contributions. Currently, for regular FERS employees,[53] agencies and USPS contribute 11.9% of pay for FERS employees first hired before 2013 and 9.6% of pay for FERS employees first hired after 2012.[54]

USPS maintains that it has made an overpayment of USPS agency contributions on behalf of its FERS employees. OPMOIG agrees that USPS has made this overpayment; it also notes that a statute would need to be enacted to authorize OPM to refund the money.[55] GAO has also concurred with this assessment.[56]

In general, USPS's FERS overpayment is a result of the significantly different composition of USPS's FERS workforce compared with FERS employees in the rest of the federal workforce. That is, the dynamic normal cost of FERS benefits for USPS employees is less than the dynamic normal cost of FERS benefits for FERS employees in the rest of the federal workforce. Currently, OPM uses the same demographic assumptions to calculate the dynamic normal costs for all FERS employees—without distinguishing between the characteristics of USPS and non-USPS employees. Current OPM estimates using the same demographic assumptions for all FERS employees, including USPS employees, yield a USPS FERS overpayment of about $3.0 billion as of FY2012:

> According to the most recent actuarial estimate received from OPM, the Postal Service had overfunded its FERS obligations by $2.6 billion at September 30, 2011, the latest actual data available. The reduction in the estimated surplus from amounts previously reported resulted primarily from changes to government-wide economic and demographic assumptions made by OPM, as well as actual fiscal year 2011 experience. OPM's most recent calculation shows that the FERS surplus was projected to grow to approximately $3.0 billion by September 30, 2012. The Office of Inspector General has reported that if Postal Service specific assumptions and demographics are used to calculate the FERS liability, rather than government-wide averages, the overfunding amount would be substantially greater.[57]

USPSOIG claims that an even larger USPS FERS overpayment would result from the use of USPS-specific demographic assumptions. According to a USPSOIG report released in September 2013,[58] using USPS-specific demographic assumptions, rather than average demographic assumptions for all FERS employees, would yield a USPS FERS overpayment of $12.5 billion for FY2012, which is $9.5 billion more than the surplus estimated by OPM using the same demographic assumptions for all FERS employees. USPSOIG's report notes the following USPSspecific demographic and other characteristics that lead to the larger USPS FERS overpayment:

- smaller pay increases for USPS employees;
- a more condensed pay scale for USPS employees;

- lower rates of service withdrawal and early retirement USPS employees;
- higher rates of in-service mortality and disability retirement for USPS employees; and
- smaller improvements in mortality for male USPS employees.

Proposals Related to USPS Pension Funding

Congress has considered a range of legislative proposals to address these two USPS pension funding issues. Four types of policy proposals have been introduced in the 113th Congress. First, there is legislation that would change the allocation of costs for CSRS benefits for certain USPS employees. Second, several pieces of legislation in the 113th Congress propose to refund the FERS overpayment to USPS. Third, there are proposals to alter the calculation of the costs of USPS FERS benefits. Finally, there has been a proposal to provide non-FERS coverage for newly hired USPS employees. Examples of these proposals are described below. *Table 2* provides summary information on these proposals.

Table 2. Examples of Legislation in the 113th Congress Related to USPS Pension Funding

Type of Proposal	Examples of Legislation Introduced in the 113th Congress
Proposals to Reallocate CSRS Costs	H.R. 630; S. 316
Proposals to Refund USPS FERS Overpayment	H.R. 630; S. 316; H.R. 961; H.R. 2690; H.R. 2748; S. 1486
Proposals to Change Calculation of USPS FERS Liabilities	H.R. 961; H.R. 2690; H.R. 2748; S. 1486
Proposals to Provide Non-FERS Coverage for New USPS Employees	S. 1486

Source: Compiled by the Congressional Research Service.

Proposals to Reallocate CSRS Costs

The House and Senate versions of the Postal Service Protection Act of 2013 (H.R. 630[59] and S. 316) both include a proposal to alter the allocation of costs of CSRS benefits for individuals with service under both USPOD and USPS.[60] H.R. 630 and S. 316 would require OPM to use final high-three pay rather than 1971 salary in calculating the federal government's portion of these CSRS benefits.[61] Any surplus created by this reallocation of CSRS costs would be transferred to the Postal Service Retiree Health Benefit Fund and the Postal Service Fund.[62]

Proposals to Refund USPS FERS Overpayment

There are also several proposals that would provide a refund of the FERS overpayment to USPS:

- The House version of the Postal Service Protection Act of 2013 (H.R. 630), would refund any USPS FERS overpayment for FY2010 to USPS.[63]
- The Senate version Postal Service Protection Act of 2013 (S. 316), would refund any USPS FERS overpayment for FY2013 to USPS.[64]
- The United States Postal Service Stabilization Act of 2013 (H.R. 961)[65] and the Innovate to Deliver Act of 2013 (H.R. 2690)[66] would refund any USPS FERS overpayment in any fiscal year in which a surplus has occurred to USPS.[67]
- The Postal Reform Act of 2013 (H.R. 2748)[68] would refund any USPS FERS overpayment in any fiscal year in which a surplus has occurred minus any USPS CSRS liability and any other federal retirement USPS liability.[69]
- The Postal Reform Act of 2013 (S. 1486) would refund any USPS FERS overpayment for FY2013 and future years to USPS.

Proposals to Change Calculation of USPS FERS Liabilities

The United States Postal Service Stabilization Act of 2013 (H.R. 961) and the Innovate to Deliver Act of 2013 (H.R. 2690) would require OPM to calculate the dynamic normal costs of USPS FERS benefits separately for USPS employees.[70]

The Postal Reform Act of 2013 (H.R. 2748) and the Postal Reform Act of 2013 (S. 1486) would require OPM to calculate a separate dynamic normal cost for USPS FERS benefits and use demographic and economic assumptions specific to USPS's workforce.[71]

Proposals to Provide Non-FERS Coverage for New USPS Employees

The Postal Reform Act of 2013 (S. 1486) would grant USPS authority to use collective bargaining to negotiate retirement benefits for new USPS employees.[72] That is, USPS employees hired after enactment of this bill may be covered by a collective bargaining agreement that provides retirement coverage not under FERS, but rather under one or more new retirement benefit plans.[73]

End Notes

[1] USPS often is mischaracterized as a quasi governmental or private entity. It is neither. USPS is a government agency that was created by Congress to achieve various public purposes. Federal law defines what products and services the Postal Service may offer. Additionally, USPS's employees are federal employees who participate in the Civil Service Retirement System, the Federal Employees Retirement System, and the Federal Employees Health Benefits Program. On quasi governmental entities, which have both governmental and private-sector attributes, see CRS Report RL30533, The Quasi Government: Hybrid Organizations with Both Government and Private Sector Legal Characteristics, by Kevin R. Kosar.

[2] PRA; P.L. 91-375; 84 Stat. 725; and 39 U.S.C. §201.

[3] The term marketized refers to a government agency structured to provide goods and services in the manner of a private firm. On marketization as an alternative to privatization, see CRS Report RL33777, Privatization and the Federal Government: An Introduction, by Kevin R. Kosar.

[4] For further details on USPS's appropriations, see CRS Report R42730, Financial Services and General Government: FY2013 Appropriations, coordinated by Garrett Hatch.

[5] 5 U.S.C. §8331 (CSRS) and 5 U.S.C. §8401 (FERS). For details on CSRS and FERS, see CRS Report 98-810, Federal Employees' Retirement System: Benefits and Financing, by Katelin P. Isaacs.

[6] 5 U.S.C. §8901(1)(A) and 5 U.S.C. §2105(e). For details on FEHBP, see CRS Report RS21974, Federal Employees Health Benefits Program (FEHBP): Available Health Insurance Options, by Annie L. Mach and Ada S. Cornell.

[7] See CRS Report R43162, The U.S. Postal Service's Financial Condition: A Primer, by Kevin R. Kosar.

[8] U.S. Postal Service, "2013 Report on Form 10-K," November 15, 2013, pp.27-28, at http://about.usps.com/who-weare/financials/10k-reports/fy2013.pdf.

[9] See Office of Personnel Management Office of the Inspector General, "A Study of the Risks and Consequences of the USPS OIG's Proposals to Change USPS's Funding of Retiree Benefits: Shifting Costs from USPS Ratepayers to Taxpayers," February 2011, p. ii, at http://archive.opm.gov/oig/ OPM_OIG_Study_of_USPS_OIG_Proposals%20Feb%2028%202011.pdf.

[10] This section was written by Kevin R. Kosar, analyst in American National Government.

[11] P.L. 109-435, §803; 120 Stat. 3251-3252; 5 U.S.C §8909(d)(3)(A).

[12] On USPS's losses, see CRS Report R43162, The U.S. Postal Service's Financial Condition: A Primer, by Kevin R. Kosar.

[13] USPS contributes to annuitants' premiums according to the formula set in statute at 5 U.S.C. §8906.

[14] In accountancy terms, PAEA requires USPS to pay annually a portion of the present value of future retiree health benefits of current employees. Thus, PAEA moved USPS from "cash accounting" to "accrual accounting." On these two approaches and their use for accounting for post-retirement benefits, see Financial Accounting Standards Board, "Summary of Statement No. 106," December 1990, at http://www.fasb.org/st/summary/stsum106.shtml. See also David M. Walker, Comptroller General, U.S. General Accounting Office, "U.S. Postal Service: Accounting for Postretirement Benefits," GAO-02-916-R, September 12, 2002, at http://www.gao.gov/assets/100/91503.pdf.

[15] CRS's review of the legislative history of PAEA did not reveal the reason(s) Congress chose to set the annual payment levels for FY2007 to FY2016 as it did, or why it enacted a 50-year payment period. GAO has stated, "The retiree health benefits payment schedule established under PAEA was significantly frontloaded, with total payment requirements through fiscal year 2016 that were significantly in excess of what actuarially determined amounts would be." U.S. Government Accountability Office, "U.S. Postal Service: Health and Pension Benefits Proposals Involve Trade-offs," GAO-13-872T, September 26, 2013, p. 4, at http://www.gao.gov/assets/660/658176.pdf.

[16] The U.S. Government Accountability Office has noted, "Contrary to statements made by some employee groups and other stakeholders, [the] PAEA did not require USPS to prefund 75 years of retiree health benefits over a 10-year period. Rather, pursuant to OPM's methodology, such payments would be projected to fund the liability over a period in excess of 50 years, from 2007 through 2056 and beyond (with rolling 15-year amortization periods after 2041)." U.S. Government Accountability Office, "U.S. Postal Service: Status, Financial Outlook, and Alternative Approaches to Fund Retiree Health Benefits," GAO-13-112, December 2012, p. 7, at http://www.gao.gov/assets/660/650511.pdf.

[17] PAEA established RHBF, an on-budget account in the U.S. Treasury. RHBF is separate from the Postal Service Fund, an off-budget account USPS uses for most of its financial transactions. For further background on the Postal Service Fund, see CRS Report RS20350, Off-Budget Status of Federal Entities: Background and Current Proposals, by Bill Heniff Jr.; and Office of Management and Budget, Budget of the U.S. Government Fiscal Year 2014, Appendix (Washington: GPO, 2013), pp. 1300-1301, at http://www.whitehouse.gov/sites/default/files/omb/budget/fy2014/assets/ oia.pdf.

[18] Prior to FY2017, USPS must pay for current retirees' health benefits from the Postal Service Fund. Beginning in FY2017, USPS is to pay these benefits from the Retiree Health Benefits Fund.

[19] Under a suspension of the rules, the House passed PAEA by a voice vote on December 8, 2006. The Senate passed PAEA without amendment by unanimous consent on December 9, 2006. The subject of prefunding has been examined by the 113th Congress. See U.S. Congress, House Oversight and Government Reform Committee, A Path Forward on Postal Reform, hearing, 113th Congress, 1st sess., July 13, 2013, at http://oversight.house.gov/hearing/a-path-forwardon-postal-reform/; and U.S. Congress, Senate Committee on Homeland Security and Governmental Affairs, Outside the Box: Reforming and Renewing the Postal Service, Part II—Promoting a 21st Century Workforce, hearing, 113th Congress, 1st session, September 26, 2013, at http://www.hsgac.senate.gov/hearings/outside-the-box-reforming-andrenewing-the-postal-service-part-ii_-promoting-a-21st-century-workforce.

[20] See Cliff Guffey, President, American Postal Workers Union, AFL-CIO, written testimony, U.S. Congress, House Oversight and Government Reform Committee, A Path Forward on Postal Reform, hearing, 113th Congress, 1st sess., July 13, 2013, p. 1, at http://oversight.house.gov/wp-content/uploads/2013/07/Guffey-Testimony-Final.pdf.

[21] Ibid.

[22] Steve Hutkins, "How the Postal Service Began Prefunding Retiree Health Care and Fell into a Deep Hole," SavethePostOffice.com, January 2, 2013, at http://www.savethepost office.com/how-postal-service-began-prefundingretiree-health-care-and-fell-deep-hole; and David Morris, "How Phantom Accounting Is Destroying the Post Office," HuffingtonPost.com, May 25, 2012, at http://www.huffingtonpost.com/david-morris/usps-budget_b_1545430.html.

[23] National Association of Letter Carriers, "Congressional Mandates and the Great Recession Have Caused the Postal Service's Recent Financial Challenges," NALC Fact Sheet, February 28, 2013, at http://www.nalc.org/depart/legpol/ pdf/USPS_financial_challenges _02-2013.pdf. Between FY2007 and FY2012, USPS paid $14.9 billion into RHBF and transferred an additional $3 billion from an escrow account. For further details, see CRS Report R43162, The U.S. Postal Service's Financial Condition: A Primer, by Kevin R. Kosar.

[24] Michael Schuyler, "Why The U.S. Postal Service Is In Greater Financial Trouble Than Most Foreign Posts—The Role of Postal Retiree Health Care Benefits," Institute for Research on the Economics of Taxation, Advisory No. 283, April 11, 2012, p. 3.

[25] U.S. Government Accountability Office, "U.S. Postal Service: Key Postal Transformation Issues," GAO-03-812T, May 29, 2003, p. 22, at http://www.gao.gov/assets/120/110008.pdf.

[26] U.S. Government Accountability Office, "U.S. Postal Service: Bold Action Needed to Continue Progress on Postal Transformation," GAO-04-108T, November 5, 2003, p. 3, at http://www.gpo.gov/fdsys/pkg/GAOREPORTS-GAO-04- 108T/pdf/GAOREPORTS-GAO-04-108T.pdf.

[27] Shortly after PAEA was enacted, USPS's chief financial officer declared, "[Prefunding] is a farsighted and responsible action that places the Postal Service in the vanguard of both the public and private sectors in providing future security for its employees, and augurs well for our long-term financial stability upon successful completion of the payments." U.S. Postal Service, "Annual Report 2007," p. 13, at http://about.usps.com/who-we-are/financials/ annual-reports/fy2007.pdf.

[28] House Committee on Oversight and Government Reform, majority, "Why the "Postal Overpayment" Is Really a Taxpayer-Funded Bailout," 112th Congress, at http://postal. oversight.house.gov/postal_surplus.html.

[29] As noted above, each year, USPS also must pay its share of the cost of its current retirees' health benefits premiums. USPS paid $2.9 billion for this expense in FY2013. U.S. Postal Service, "2013 Report on Form 10-K," p. 27.

[30] CRS Report R43162, The U.S. Postal Service's Financial Condition: A Primer, by Kevin R. Kosar.

[31] Ibid, pp. 8-9; and 39 U.S.C. §2005(a).

[32] U.S. Postal Service, "Quarter III, 2013 Report on Form 10-Q," p. 8, at https://about.usps.com/who-we-are/financials/ financial-conditions-results-reports/fy2013-q3.pdf.

[33] U.S. Postal Service, "2012 Report on Form 10-K," p. 43, at http://about.usps.com/who-we-are/financials/10k-reports/ fy2012.pdf.

[34] Ibid, p. 43.

[35] As noted earlier in this report, PAEA set fixed annual RHBF payment rates for the years FY2007 to FY2016. After that time, the annual payment amounts are to be determined based upon OPM's calculation of USPS's total retiree health benefits obligation, which PAEA requires to be retired by FY2056.

[36] U.S. Postal Service Inspector General, Final Management Advisory Report–Estimates of Postal Service Liability for Retiree Health Care Benefits (Washington: USPSOIG, July 22, 2009), at http://www.uspsoig.gov/foia_files/ESS-MA09-001R.pdf; and Postal Regulatory Commission, Postal Regulatory Commission Review of Retiree Health Benefit Fund Liability as Calculated by Office of Personnel Management and U.S. Postal Service Office of Inspector General (Washington: PRC, July 30, 2009), p. 22, at http://www.prc.gov/Docs/63/63987/ Retiree%20Health%20Fund%20Study_109.pdf. See also written testimony of David C. Williams, Inspector General, U.S. Postal Service Office of Inspector General, in U.S. Congress, Senate Committee on Homeland Security and Governmental Affairs, Subcommittee on Federal Financial Management, Government Information, Federal Services, and International Security, The U.S. Postal Service in Crisis, 111th Cong., 1st sess., S. Hrg. 111-409 (Washington: GPO, 2010), pp. 83-87, at http://www.gpo.gov/fdsys/pkg/CHRG-111shrg53836/pdf/CHRG-111shrg53836.pdf.

[37] Postal Regulatory Commission, Postal Regulatory Commission Review of Retiree Health Benefit Fund Liability as Calculated by Office of Personnel Management and U.S. Postal Service Office of Inspector General, p. 3. Since FY2007, USPS's permanent workforce has become smaller, decreasing from approximately 685,000 to 491,000. U.S. Postal Service, "2013 Report on Form 10-K," p.29.

[38] This list is intended to be representative of the approaches being considered by the 113th Congress, and not an exhaustive list of legislation introduced.

[39] Introduced by Rep. DeFazio on April 8, 2013; and introduced by Sen. Sanders on February 13, 2013, respectively.

[40] Introduced by Rep. Cummings on July 16, 2013. Rep. Cummings is the ranking Member of the House Oversight and Government Reform Committee, which has jurisdiction over postal issues.

[41] Introduced by Rep. Issa on July 19, 2013, and reported by the House Oversight and Government Reform Committee on July 24, 2013. Rep. Issa is the chairman of the House Oversight and Government Reform Committee.

[42] Introduced by Sen. Carper on August 1, 2013. Senator is the chairman of the Senate Homeland Security and Governmental Affairs Committee, which has jurisdiction over postal issues. S. 1486 is co-sponsored by Sen. Coburn, who is the ranking Member.

[43] This section was written by Katelin P. Isaacs, Analyst in Income Security.

[44] For additional background on CSRS, including eligibility requirements and benefit calculations, see CRS Report 98- 810, Federal Employees' Retirement System: Benefits and Financing, by Katelin P. Isaacs.

[45] 88 Stat. 354. CSRS benefit calculations are based, in part, on a measure of pay: "high-three" pay, which is defined as the highest three consecutive years of basic pay (5 U.S.C. §8331(4)). Because salary tends to rise across the course of a career, for most USPS employees and other federal employees, the most recent three years of service will produce the high-three pay measure. For more details on CSRS benefits, see CRS Report 98-810, Federal Employees' Retirement System: Benefits and Financing, by Katelin P. Isaacs.

[46] 117 Stat. 624. Actuaries use the term "dynamic normal cost" to refer to the amount, expressed as a percentage of payroll, that must be set aside each year to fund pension benefits for workers who will continue to accrue new benefits, including the effects of employee pay raises, post-retirement COLAs, and changes in the rate of interest.

[47] United States Postal Service, Office of Inspector General, The Postal Service's Share of CSRS Pension Responsibility, RARC-WP-10-001, January 20, 2010, at http://www.uspsoig.gov/sites/default/files/document-libraryfiles/2013/RARC-WP-10-001.pdf.

[48] Postal Regulatory Commission, Report to the Postal Regulatory Commission on: Civil Service Retirement System Cost and Benefit Allocation Principles, by the Segal Group, Inc., June 29, 2010, at http://www.prc.gov/Docs/68/68679/ Report%20on%20CSRS% 20Cost%20 and%20Benefit%20Allocation%20Principles_1126.pdf.

[49] The benefit accrual rate for CSRS annuities is 1.5% for the first five years of service; 1.75% for years 6 through 10; and 2.0% for any years of service after 10 years. For a more detailed illustration of the alternative methods of allocating CSRS benefits costs between the federal government and USPS under the PRC and USPSOIG proposals, see Table 3 in U.S. Government Accountability Office, U.S. Postal Service: Allocation of Responsibility for Pension Benefits between the Postal Service and the Federal Government, GAO-12-146, October 2011, pp. 6-7, at http://www.gao.gov/assets/ 590/585739.pdf.

[50] Office of Personnel Management Office of Inspector General, "A Study of the Risks and Consequences of the USPS OIG's Proposals to Change USPS's Funding of Retiree Benefits."

[51] U.S. Government Accountability Office, U.S. Postal Service: Allocation of Responsibility for Pension Benefits between the Postal Service and the Federal Government, GAO-12-146, October 2011, pp. 6-7, at http://www.gao.gov/ assets/590/585739.pdf.

[52] For additional background on FERS, including eligibility requirements and benefit calculations, see CRS Report 98- 810, Federal Employees' Retirement System: Benefits and Financing, by Katelin P. Isaacs.

[53] "Regular" FERS employees are individuals that are not "special category" employees such as Members of Congress, congressional employees, or federal law enforcement officers.

[54] The decreased agency contributions and increased employee contributions for employees hired after 2012 were enacted under P.L. 112-96.

[55] Office of Personnel Management Office of Inspector General, "A Study of the Risks and Consequences of the USPS OIG's Proposals to Change USPS's Funding of Retiree Benefits," pp. 22-25.

[56] U.S. Government Accountability Office, U.S. Postal Service: Allocation of Responsibility for Pension Benefits between the Postal Service and the Federal Government, Appendix II.

[57] United State Postal Service, "Form 10-Q: Quarter III, 2013," p. 15.

[58] United States Postal Service, Office of Inspector General, The Using U.S. Postal Service-Specific Assumptions for Calculating the Federal Employees Retirement System Liability, FT-MA-13-024, September 27, 2013, at http://www.uspsoig.gov/sites/default/files/ document-library-files/2013/ft-ma-13-024.pdf.

[59] Introduced by Rep. DeFazio on February 13, 2013.

[60] See Section 101 in both H.R. 630 and S. 316.

[61] This proposal follows the recommendations made in the 2010 Postal Regulatory Commission report. See Postal Regulatory Commission, Report to the Postal Regulatory Commission on: Civil Service Retirement System Cost and Benefit Allocation Principles, by the Segal Group, Inc., June 29, 2010.

[62] The Postal Service Fund is authorized under Section 2003 of Title 39 of U.S. Code.

[63] H.R. 630, Section 103. The FERS overpayment fund would be transferred, at the request of USPS, to (1) the Postal Service Retiree Health Benefit Fund; (2) the Postal Service Fund (established by 39 U.S.C. §2003; (3) the Postal Service Employees' Compensation Fund (established by 5 U.S.C. §8147 to fund workers' compensation benefits for USPS employees); and (4) USPS to repay debt obligations under 39 U.S.C. §2005.

[64] S. 316, Section 103. The FERS overpayment fund would be transferred, at the request of USPS, in the same ways as by H.R. 630, Section 103. See footnote 63.

[65] Introduced by Rep. Lynch on March 5, 2013.

[66] Introduced by Rep. Cummings on July 16, 2013.

[67] H.R. 961, Section 3 and H.R. 2690, Section 202. Under these proposals, the FERS overpayment fund would be transferred in the first year that such a surplus is determined to USPS to repay debt obligations under 39 U.S.C. §2005. Any USPS FERS surplus in future fiscal years would be transferred to the CSRDF to fund USPS CSRS liabilities.

[68] Introduced by Rep. Issa on July 19, 2013.

[69] H.R. 2748, Section 501. Any USPS FERS overpayment refund would be transferred to the Postal Service Retiree Health Benefit Fund.

[70] H.R. 961, Section 2 and H.R. 2690, Section 201. These proposals do not specify that OPM would use USPS-specific demographic assumptions for this calculation—just that the dynamic normal costs of FERS benefits be calculated separately for USPS employees.

[71] H.R. 2748, Section 505 and S. 1486, Section 101. Both of these sections in H.R. 2748 and S. 1486 would also require OPM to redetermine a USPS liability or surplus for CSRS employees using demographic and economic assumptions specific to USPS's workforce.

[72] S. 1486, Section 102.

[73] This proposal would also authorize collective bargaining on the required retirement contributions for new USPS employees as well as whether USPS would make employer matching contribution to the Thrift Savings Plan (TSP) accounts of new employees (and if so, how much these employer matching contributions will be). For an overview of the TSP, including current employer matching contributions for FERS employees, see CRS Report RL30387, Federal Employees' Retirement System: The Role of the Thrift Savings Plan, by Katelin P. Isaacs.

In: U.S. Postal Service Reform
Editor: Martin Thomas
ISBN: 978-1-53610-463-9

Chapter 4

U.S. POSTAL SERVICE: POST OFFICE CHANGES SUGGEST COST SAVINGS, BUT IMPROVED GUIDANCE, DATA, AND ANALYSIS CAN INFORM FUTURE SAVINGS EFFORTS*

United States Government Accountability Office

WHY GAO DID THIS STUDY

USPS continues to experience a financial crisis and has undertaken many initiatives to reduce costs. In May 2012, USPS announced POStPlan, which aimed to reduce retail hours at post offices and use less costly labor. However, an arbitrator ruled in September 2014 that USPS must reverse several of these staffing changes. GAO was asked to review the arbitration decision's effects on POStPlan staffing and cost savings.

GAO examined: (1) USPS's actions to implement POStPlan before the decision and expected savings, (2) the decision's effects on POStPlan's staffing and savings, and (3) whether USPS's POStPlan cost-savings estimates are reliable. GAO reviewed relevant POStPlan documentation and data; compared USPS's POStPlan cost-savings estimating process to GAO's data

* This is an edited, reformatted and augmented version of a United States Government Accountability Office Publication No. GAO-16-385, dated April 2016.

reliability and cost- estimating guidance and internal control standards adopted by USPS; and interviewed officials from USPS, its regulatory body, and postmaster associations.

WHAT GAO RECOMMENDS

To ensure that USPS has quality information regarding POStPlan, GAO recommends that USPS establish guidance that clarifies when to develop savings estimates using a rigorous approach; resolve errors in labor data and, as appropriate, recalculate actual savings achieved; and take steps to improve revenue analyses. USPS disagreed with some of GAO's findings but neither agreed or disagreed with the recommendations. GAO continues to believe its recommendations are valid as discussed further in this report.

WHAT GAO FOUND

The U.S. Postal Service (USPS) had largely completed Post Office Structure Plan's (POStPlan) implementation prior to a 2014 POStPlan arbitration decision and expected millions in cost savings. Specifically, under POStPlan, USPS planned to reduce hours at about 13,000 post offices (from 8- to 2-, 4-, or 6-hours of retail service a day) and to staff them with employees less costly than postmasters. Prior to the arbitration decision, USPS had reduced hours at most of these offices and taken steps to make the staffing changes. For example, it replaced many career postmasters with non-career or part-time employees by offering separation incentives or reassignments. In July 2012, USPS estimated POStPlan would result in about $500 million in annual cost savings.

USPS determined that, while the 2014 arbitration decision significantly affected planned staffing at POStPlan post offices and estimated savings, POStPlan was the correct operational decision for USPS and its stakeholders. The arbitrator ruled that many offices be staffed by bargaining-unit employees, such as clerks, rather than the generally less costly employees USPS had planned to use. As a result, USPS estimated in June 2015 that POStPlan would now result in annual savings of about $337 million or 35 percent less than the about $500 million it expected.

USPS's original and post-arbitration decision estimates of expected POStPlan cost savings have limitations that affect their reliability. USPS officials noted that they do not have strict guidance on when a rough savings estimate is adequate versus when a more rigorous analysis is appropriate. Specific limitations include:

- imprecise and incomplete labor costs, including errors in underlying data;
- lack of a sensitivity review; and
- the exclusion of other factors that affect *net* cost savings, particularly the potential impact of reduced retail hours on revenue.

For example, USPS's post-arbitration-decision estimate relies, in part, on its calculations of actual savings achieved due to POStPlan. While POStPlan most likely resulted in some savings, GAO found errors in the underlying salaries and benefits data used that may understate or overstate the amount of savings achieved. Additionally, while USPS later (i.e., after it developed its savings estimates) conducted analyses of changes in revenue, GAO found these analyses were limited because USPS's calculations of changes in revenue at POStPlan and non-POStPlan post offices were inconsistent with its definition of what constitutes a POStPlan office. As of March 2016, USPS was taking steps to understand the scope and origin of the errors in its salaries and benefits data, but its time frame for resolving the issue remains unclear, as does whether USPS subsequently intends to update its calculations of actual savings achieved. Internal control standards state that program managers and decision makers need quality data and information to determine whether they are meeting their goals. Without reliable data and quality methods for calculating the potential savings USPS expects to achieve through its initiatives, the actual savings they achieve, and the effects on revenue, USPS officials and oversight bodies may lack accurate and relevant information with which to make informed decisions regarding future cost-saving efforts in a time of constrained resources.

ABBREVIATIONS

APWU	American Postal Workers Union
CBA	collective bargaining agreement

COSO	Committee of Sponsoring Organizations of the Treadway Commission
EPM	Evaluated Postmaster
FY	fiscal year
NAPUS	National Association of Postmasters of the United States
NLPM	National League of Postmasters of the United States
NTFT	Non-Traditional Full-Time
OMB	Office of Management and Budget
PMR	Postmaster Relief
POStPlan	Post Office Structure Plan
PRC	Postal Regulatory Commission
PSE	Postal Support Employee
PTF	Part-Time Flexible
PTPO	part time post office
RIF	reduction in force
RMPO	remotely managed post office
USPS	U.S. Postal Service

* * *

April 29, 2016

The Honorable Jason Chaffetz
Chairman
Committee on Oversight and Government Reform
House of Representatives

The Honorable Mark Meadows
Chairman
Subcommittee on Government Operations
Committee on Oversight and Government Reform
House of Representatives

The U.S. Postal Service (USPS) continues to experience a serious financial crisis with, as of fiscal year 2015, nine consecutive years of large net losses, about $125 billion in unfunded liabilities,[1] no further authority to borrow from the U.S. Treasury,[2] and expected continued declines in mail volume that will affect revenue. The task of restructuring USPS to achieve sustainable financial viability has been on our list of high-risk areas since

2009, and we have reported that USPS urgently needs to restructure to align its costs with revenues.[3] To improve its financial condition while working to meet its statutory mission of providing prompt, reliable, and efficient service to all areas of the country,[4] USPS has undertaken a number of initiatives to right-size its retail network.[5] In particular, in May 2012, USPS announced the Post Office Structure Plan (POStPlan) initiative, through which it aimed to reduce the retail hours at thousands of mostly small, rural post offices and staff them with lower paid employees. However, in response to a filed labor grievance, an impartial arbitrator ruled in September 2014 that USPS must reverse several of the planned staffing changes. You asked us to review the arbitration decision's effects on POStPlan staffing and estimated cost savings. This report examines (1) the actions USPS took to implement POStPlan before the September 2014 arbitration decision and the savings it estimated POStPlan would achieve, (2) the effect USPS determined the arbitration decision had on POStPlan staffing and cost savings, and (3) whether USPS's POStPlan cost-savings estimates are reliable and any limitations of the estimates.

To describe the POStPlan initiative, determine the actions USPS took to implement it before the September 2014 arbitration decision and to identify the effects USPS determined that the decision had on POStPlan staffing, we reviewed relevant laws, regulations, and USPS documentation, such as policies, procedures, and information submitted during the Postal Regulatory Commission's (PRC) 2012 POStPlan proceeding.[6] We also reviewed the arbitration decision and subsequent memorandums of understanding that further implemented it.[7] In addition, we obtained USPS data related to the arbitration decision and POStPlan implementation from 2012 to 2015 and interviewed USPS officials. We assessed the reliability of these data by comparing them to other information obtained from USPS and asking USPS officials questions about data sources, quality, and timeliness. We found these data reliable for the purpose of describing the progress and status of POStPlan before and after the arbitration decision. To obtain their views on POStPlan and the arbitration decision, we also reviewed documentation and interviewed officials from PRC and USPS's two postmaster associations—the National Association of Postmasters of the United States (NAPUS) and the National League of Postmasters of the United States (NLPM). For example, we reviewed PRC's 2012 advisory opinion on POStPlan.[8] We also contacted the American Postal Workers Union (APWU), but APWU officials did not accept our invitation for a meeting.[9]

To determine the cost savings USPS originally estimated it would achieve through POStPlan, the effect it estimated the arbitration decision had on savings, and the reliability and limitations of these estimates, we reviewed USPS's 2012 estimate of the cost savings it expected to achieve through POStPlan and its 2015 estimate of the arbitration decision's impact on expected cost savings. Specifically, we obtained USPS documentation related to POStPlan cost savings, interviewed USPS officials, and obtained documentation and interviewed officials from NAPUS, NLPM, and PRC to determine how USPS developed its estimates, the assumptions it used, the potential sources of uncertainty, the types of inputs included and omitted, and these stakeholders' views. We then assessed the reliability and soundness of these estimates using our guidance on assessing the reliability of data (the guidance defines data as including estimates—such as estimates of cost savings—and projections),[10] our cost-estimating guidance and that from the Office of Management and Budget (OMB),[11] and internal control standards adopted by USPS.[12] We reviewed these standards and guidance and then selected those practices that, in our professional judgment, were most relevant given that POStPlan is an efficiency and cost-savings initiative and given USPS's financial condition. In particular, we assessed the estimates' accuracy, validity, completeness, and consistency; any use of sensitivity analyses; and consideration of net cost-savings factors. We also obtained USPS data on hourly pay rates in POStPlan post offices pre- and post-arbitration decision; salaries and benefits paid, and walk-in revenue earned, at POStPlan post offices for periods before (fiscal year 2011) and after (during fiscal year 2015) POStPlan implementation; and actual cost savings achieved from fiscal year 2012 to June 2015 (the most recent data available at the time of our review) due to POStPlan.[13] We assessed the reliability of these data by comparing them to other information obtained from USPS and asking USPS questions about data sources, quality, and timeliness, among other things. We found USPS's rate and revenue data reliable for the purpose of describing the hourly pay rates in POStPlan post offices according to USPS and the changes in revenue at POStPlan post offices. We discuss the limitations of USPS's salaries and benefits and actual savings achieved data in this report. It was beyond the scope of our review to assess whether POStPlan was a prudent business decision. Appendix I describes our scope and methodology in greater detail.

We conducted this performance audit from May 2015 to April 2016 in accordance with generally accepted government auditing standards.

Those standards require that we plan and perform the audit to obtain sufficient, appropriate evidence to provide a reasonable basis for our findings and conclusions based on our audit objectives. We believe that the evidence obtained provides a reasonable basis for our findings and conclusions based on our audit objectives.

BACKGROUND

The USPS Retail Network and Workforce

The most familiar part of USPS's retail network is the post office. In fiscal year 2015, there were approximately 26,600 post offices across the country, largely unchanged from fiscal year 2005 (see fig. 1). Post offices are a key part of USPS's revenue stream—accounting for about 56 percent of USPS's total retail revenue of about $19 billion in fiscal year 2015.[14] Prior to the introduction of POStPlan, post offices were each managed by postmasters. USPS also uses other facilities to provide key services, such as selling stamps.

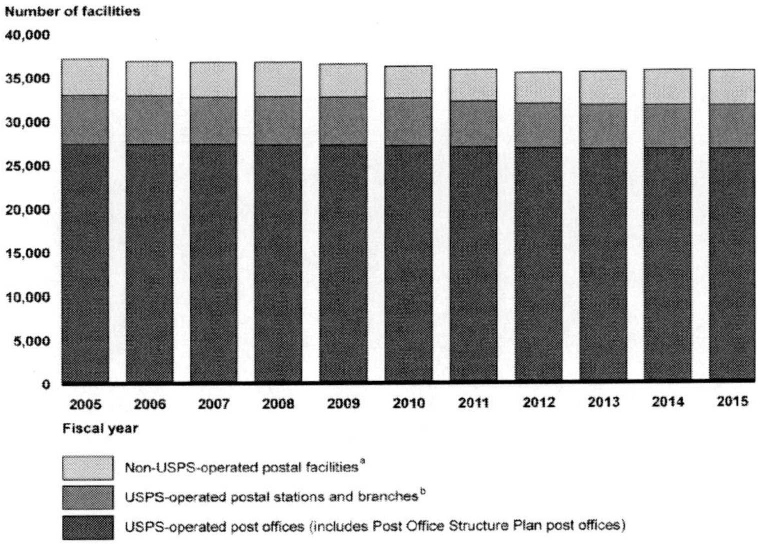

Source: U.S. Postal Service (USPS) data. | GAO-16-385.

[a] Non-USPS-operated postal facilities include Contract Postal Units and Village and Community Post Offices operated by non-postal employees in privately operated businesses, such as convenience and grocery stores.

[b] Postal stations and branches are facilities subordinate to a local post office located within and outside, respectively, a municipality's corporate limits.

Figure 1. Number of Postal Retail Facilities, Fiscal Years 2005-2015.

Over the past decade, the USPS workforce has declined and changed in composition, but continues to account for almost 80 percent of USPS's total operating costs ($58 of $74 billion in fiscal year 2015).[15] From fiscal years 2005 to 2015, USPS's workforce decreased from 803,000 to approximately 622,000 employees, or by about 23 percent (see fig. 2).

During this period, career employees decreased (from approximately 704,700 to 491,900 or by about 30 percent), while non-career employees increased (from approximately 98,300 to 130,000 or by about 32 percent). Career positions—which are generally full time but also may be parttime—are eligible for annual and sick leave, health insurance, life insurance, and retirement benefits. Non-career employees supplement the career workforce and receive lower wages. They are not eligible for life insurance or retirement benefits, but some are eligible for specified types of health insurance upon hiring while others are eligible after serving at least 1 year.

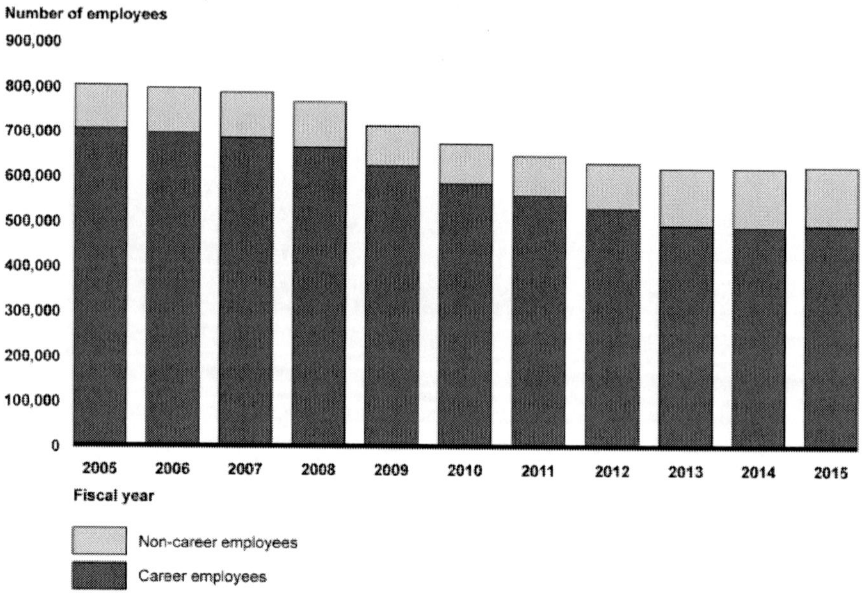

Source: USPS data. | GAO-16-385.

Figure 2. Number of U.S. Postal Service (USPS) Employees, Fiscal Years 2005-2015.

About 90 percent of USPS's career employees—and some types of non-career employees, such as Postal Support Employees—are covered by collective bargaining agreements and represented through unions.[16] APWU, one of USPS's largest unions, represents over 200,000 USPS employees in the clerk, maintenance, motor vehicle, and support services employee "crafts." The USPS-APWU 2010-2015 Collective Bargaining Agreement (CBA) contains various provisions that specify rules associated with the performance of bargaining-unit work (such as staffing the retail window and placing mail in customers' post office boxes) by USPS employees. For example, the agreement specifies that USPS should assign new or revised positions that contain non-supervisory duties to the most appropriate employee craft and that USPS should consult with APWU before doing so.

Two associations represent USPS's postmasters, who are not covered by CBAs: NAPUS and NLPM.[17] USPS is required to consult with these associations on planning, developing, and implementing certain programs and policies—like POStPlan—that affect them.[18]

The POStPlan Initiative

In May 2012, USPS announced the POStPlan initiative. POStPlan sought to right-size USPS's retail network of—at the time—26,703 post offices. Generally, POStPlan had two elements:

- reduce retail window service hours at some offices to better match actual customer use, and
- change the staffing arrangements at those offices to reduce labor costs.[19]

According to USPS officials, they informed APWU of POStPlan in May 2012, after announcing the initiative.

To evaluate which offices may be appropriate for hour reductions, in December 2011, USPS analyzed the daily workload—as a proxy for customer use—at 17,728 offices.[20] Through this analysis, USPS determined that it could reduce hours at 13,167 of these offices from 8- to 2-, 4-, or 6-hours of retail service a day. Post offices are classified into "levels" and, under POStPlan, these reduced-hour offices would be classified into a new set of levels that correspond with the number of hours of retail service they would provide per day (i.e., Level 2, Level 4, and Level 6). USPS also determined that the remaining 4,561 offices it analyzed should continue to provide 8 hours of retail service a day; USPS classified these offices as Level 18 offices.[21]

USPS planned for most of the reduced-hour offices to be managed remotely. That is, under POStPlan, Level 2, 4, and 6 offices would be considered "remotely managed post offices" (RMPO) and they would report to a postmaster at a Level 18 or above "administrative" post office.[22] USPS created an exception for offices it considered especially isolated. These offices would not be remotely managed and would, instead, be called "part time post offices" (PTPO); all PTPOs would be Level 6 offices.[23] According to USPS officials, Level 2, 4, and 6 RMPOs and PTPOs are the "POStPlan post offices;" Level 18 or above offices are not considered POStPlan post offices.

USPS plans to review workloads at POStPlan RMPOs annually and, based on these reviews, may increase or decrease the number of hours of retail service at these offices. USPS also plans to review the workload at the Level 18 and above offices through USPS's separate, prePOStPlan processes, and based on the results, USPS may designate any qualifying office a POStPlan post office and reduce its hours accordingly if its workload justifies a reduction in hours.[24]

Regarding the staffing arrangements at these offices, USPS planned to replace career postmasters in the POStPlan post offices with less costly non-career or part-time employees, as shown in fig. 3. Level 18 offices would continue to be staffed by career, full-time postmasters.

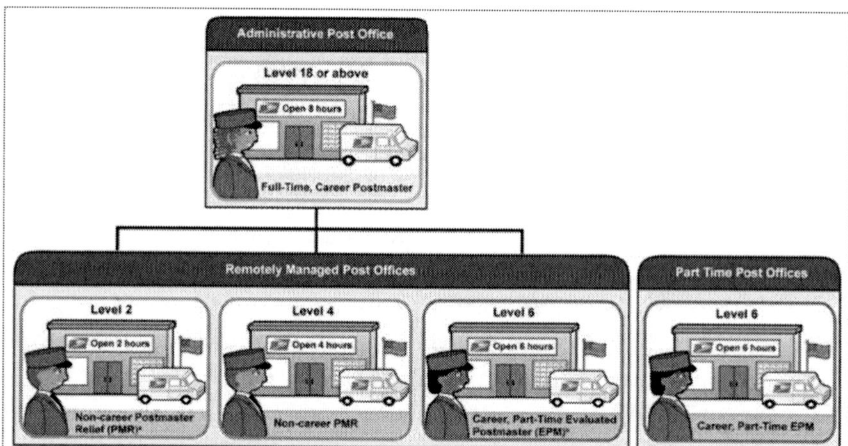

Source: GAO based on USPS information. | GAO-16-385.

[a]PMRs are employees who serve as a relief or leave replacement during the absence of a postmaster in certain post offices.

[b]EPMs are career postmasters employed by USPS in a capacity that is less than full time.

Figure 3. U.S. Postal Service's (USPS) Post Office Structure Plan (POStPlan) Staffing Arrangements as Originally Proposed in May 2012.

On July 9, 2012, APWU filed a labor grievance claiming the changes introduced by POStPlan violated provisions of the USPS-APWU 2010- 2015 CBA. USPS officials said they had the authority to modify the POStPlan initiative during the grievance procedure but decided to proceed with POStPlan implementation because they believed it was the proper operational decision for its customers, employees, and USPS. As a result, USPS continued with POStPlan implementation until September 2014, when—as discussed later in this report—an independent arbitrator issued a decision that resolved the grievance.

USPS Had Largely Completed POStPlan Implementation Prior to the Arbitration Decision and Expected Total Cost Savings of $500 Million Annually

USPS Took Steps to Modify Retail Hours and Staffing at Most POStPlan Post Offices

Prior to the issuance of the POStPlan arbitration decision in September 2014, USPS had taken steps to reduce hours at almost three-quarters of POStPlan post offices. After announcing POStPlan in May 2012, USPS began implementation by reviewing its determinations on: (1) which offices would have reduced hours, (2) which were considered especially isolated, (3) which would be reclassified as Level 18, and (4) which would become administrative offices. In July 2012, USPS finalized those decisions and communicated the results to relevant field personnel, who had the opportunity to advise on any potential concerns that could not be identified at the USPS headquarters level.[25] In September 2012, USPS began surveying residents of the affected communities to give them an opportunity to provide input before reducing their office's hours.[26] The survey asked whether they preferred USPS continue with its plan to reduce hours or whether they preferred USPS close their office and institute alternatives, such as relocating post office box service to a nearby office. In October 2012, USPS began holding meetings in the communities to communicate the survey results and consider feedback. Thereafter, USPS continued to conduct meetings and reduce hours at offices on a rolling basis, with the first reductions occurring in November 2012 and most occurring within the first year of POStPlan's announcement (see fig. 4). Specifically, from November 2012 through August 2014, USPS reduced hours at 9,159 post offices, or at about 72 percent of the almost 12,800 that would ultimately have hours reduced under POStPlan.[27]

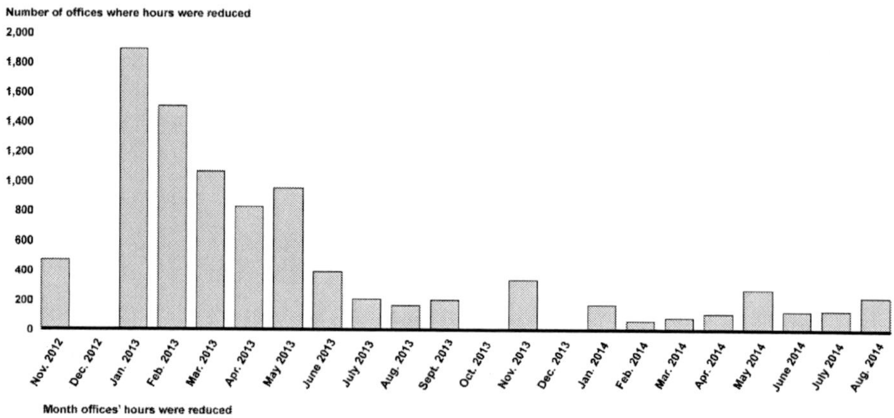

Source: USPS data. | GAO-16-385.

Figure 4. Implementation of the U.S. Postal Service (USPS) Post Office Structure Plan at Post Offices through August 2014.

According to USPS officials, they implemented POStPlan on a rolling basis to make building modifications to some offices (to ensure that customers could maintain access to their post office box even with reduced hours) and to minimize the effect on POStPlan-affected postmasters. For example, implementing POStPlan on a rolling basis allowed affected postmasters more time to find reassignment opportunities, as described below.

In addition to reducing hours at over 9,000 of the POStPlan post offices, USPS simultaneously took steps to make the necessary staffing changes and provide options for postmasters to separate from USPS or be reassigned to other positions ahead of a planned "reduction in force" (RIF). USPS announced a $20,000 separation incentive offer for all postmasters in May 2012, followed by a $10,000 offer in July 2014 to those POStPlan-affected postmasters who did not accept the first incentive offer. In May 2012, USPS also began periodically posting vacancies that POStPlan-affected postmasters could apply to, such as positions that became available as postmasters retired through the May 2012 separation incentive. Postmasters in offices set to become Level 6 offices could also opt to remain in their office and accept a demotion to the new, part-time position. According to USPS officials, as postmasters separated from USPS or accepted reassignments, USPS filled the positions according to its new POStPlan staffing arrangements. USPS initially intended to complete POStPlan implementation by September 2014, with any POStPlan-affected postmasters who had not separated from USPS or been reassigned to an alternate position as of this date to be separated via RIF. However, USPS extended this deadline twice during implementation—first to January then February of 2015—in order to, according to USPS officials, find reassignment opportunities for as many POStPlan-affected postmasters as possible. By September 2014, about 4,100 POStPlan-affected postmasters had separated from USPS[28] and about 5,800 had been reassigned to a different position.[29]

USPS Estimated Cost Savings of about $500 Million Annually Following Full POStPlan Implementation

In July 2012, USPS estimated it would achieve $516 million annually in labor cost savings once POStPlan had been fully implemented for a complete year (that is, once retail hours had been adjusted in all POStPlan post offices). Given that USPS originally intended to complete implementation by September 2014, this means the program would have been implemented for a complete year in September 2015, with full annual cost savings beginning in fiscal year 2016.

To develop this estimate, USPS calculated "before POStPlan" and "after POStPlan" labor costs at the approximately 13,000 POStPlan post offices and at the Level 18 offices using average salary and benefits data as of pay period 6 of fiscal year 2012. To arrive at the "before POStPlan" labor cost, USPS multiplied the number of post offices at each applicable, prePOStPlan office level by the average salary and benefits that career postmasters at those levels earn, then totaled the results. To arrive at the "after POStPlan" labor cost, USPS multiplied the number of offices at each post-POStPlan office level by the projected salary and benefits it expected for employees that would staff those offices (based on the new POStPlan staffing arrangements) then totaled the results. The $516 million represents the difference between these "before" and "after" calculations. In June 2015, USPS revised this original estimate to $518 million in annual labor cost savings based on: (1) the actual savings it estimated it achieved from fiscal years 2012 to 2014, (2) the remaining savings it expected to achieve from offices whose hours had been reduced in the prior year, and (3) the savings it expected to achieve from offices whose hours had not yet been reduced.

USPS Determined the 2014 Arbitration Decision Significantly Affected POStPlan Staffing and Expected Cost Savings

The Arbitration Decision Changed Planned Staffing at About 82 Percent of POStPlan Post Offices

On September 5, 2014, an impartial arbitrator resolved APWU's POStPlan grievance and ruled that the staffing changes introduced by POStPlan violated certain provisions of the USPS-APWU 2010-2015 CBA, and that USPS must reverse several of these changes.[30] The arbitrator agreed with APWU's argument that, under POStPlan, employees in Level 4 and 6 RMPOs were no longer performing any managerial or supervisory work and also that the work was clerical in nature and should be assigned to bargaining-unit employees.[31] As a result, according to USPS officials, the arbitration decision significantly changed staffing in these offices, which account for about 82 percent of POStPlan post offices as of August 2015, by awarding all non-bargainingunit positions in them to APWU-represented employees. The arbitrator's decision on staffing in Level 4 RMPOs also affected the resolution of a separate dispute. Specifically, in the POStPlan arbitration decision, the arbitrator also ruled on a dispute regarding the type of work assignments that staff in Level 18 offices could perform, finding certain Level 18 offices must be staffed by a career employee (see fig. 5). USPS continued to modify hours at POStPlan post offices as these changes were taking place. According to USPS officials, subsequent memorandums of understanding between USPS and APWU mitigated some of what the officials believe could have been potentially negative effects of the arbitration decision.

According to USPS officials as of February 2016, staffing changes related to POStPlan and the arbitration decision are complete. USPS, NAPUS, and NLPM officials told us that managing employee work rules under the post-arbitration staffing arrangements is more complex than under the original POStPlan staffing arrangements. They noted that this is because each employee category has different work rules to manage and there were fewer employee categories under the original POStPlan staffing arrangements.[32]

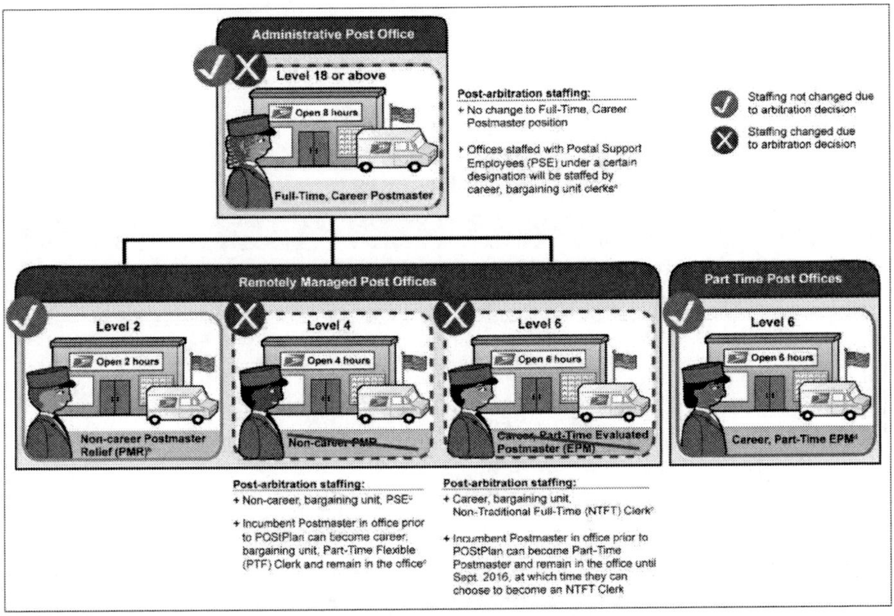

Source: GAO based on USPS information. | GAO-16-385.

[a]Because postmasters in Level 18 offices are not authorized to perform more than 15 hours per week of bargaining-unit work, USPS must staff these offices with either PTF or NTFT clerks who will perform any bargaining-unit work in excess of this limit.

[b]PMRs are employees who serve as a relief or leave replacement during the absence of a postmaster in certain post offices.

[c]PSE, PTF, and NTFT are categories of employees who are available to work flexible hours as assigned by USPS.

[d]EPMs are career postmasters employed by USPS in a capacity that is less than full-time.

Figure 5. U.S. Postal Service's (USPS) Post Office Structure Plan (POStPlan) Staffing Arrangements after the September 2014 POStPlan Arbitration Decision.

USPS Estimated the Arbitration Decision Will Reduce Originally Expected Cost Savings by Over a Third

USPS estimated that, due to the arbitration decision, annual POStPlan cost savings will be lower than originally expected. Specifically, in June 2015, USPS estimated that the decision will reduce estimated annual cost savings by $181 million, which is approximately 35 percent less than the revised estimate of $518 million. As a result, USPS projected that POStPlan will now result in total annual labor cost savings of about $337 million.

POStPlan post office category	Staffing	Minimum & maximum hourly rate with benefits, as of August 2015	Fiscal year 2015 actual average hourly rate with benefits
Remotely Managed Post Office			
Level 2	Postmaster Relief (PMR)	$13.42 – $21.70	$14.87
	No change to staffing due to arbitration		
Level 4	PMR	$13.42 – $21.70	$14.87
	Postal Support Employee (PSE)	N/A	$18.16
	Part-Time Flexible (PTF) Clerk	$34.48 – $44.69 (Tier 1)[a] $26.53 – $36.18 (Tier 2)	$44.67 (Tier 1) $27.78 (Tier 2)
Level 6	Evaluated Postmaster (EPM)	$14.81 – $21.70	$21.17[b]
	Non-Traditional Full-Time (NTFT) Clerk	$35.47 – $49.02 (Tier 1) $27.27 – $40.52 (Tier 2)	$45.03 (Tier 1) $28.87 (Tier 2)
	Incumbent, Part-Time Postmaster	$13.42 – $33.29	$32.59[c]
Part Time Post Office			
Level 6	EPM	$14.81 – $21.70	$21.17
	No change to staffing due to arbitration		

Legend: Originally proposed POStPlan staffing arrangements; Post-arbitration POStPlan staffing arrangements

Source: GAO based on USPS information. | GAO-16-385.

[a]USPS divides PTF and NTFT employees into two tiers based on when they were converted from non-career to career employees.

[b]Although not part of the originally proposed POStPlan staffing arrangements, according to USPS officials some PSEs also staffed these offices prior to the arbitration decision, and PSEs' fiscal year 2015 actual average hourly rate with benefits was $18.16.

[c]This is an estimated rate calculated by USPS officials because USPS did not have specific categories of this data in its system.

Figure 6. U.S. Postal Service's (USPS) Post Office Structure Plan (POStPlan) Employee Compensation before and after the September 2014 POStPlan Arbitration Decision.

To develop the estimate of the impact from the arbitration decision, USPS used a slightly different approach than it had used to develop its original cost-savings estimate. Specifically, USPS calculated the difference between the hourly salary and benefit rates for employees in the Level 4 and 6 POStPlan post offices under the original, pre-arbitration POStPlan staffing arrangements and under the post-arbitration POStPlan staffing arrangements. It then multiplied the rate differences by the total hours worked per year at the applicable offices and totaled the results. This resulted in a difference of $181 million. USPS then subtracted the $181 million from the $518 million in annual savings it expected to achieve to arrive at the revised estimated annual savings of $337 million. According to USPS officials, USPS developed this estimate using a different approach from its original POStPlan cost-savings estimate because the arbitration decision resulted in a new labor type and rate and USPS believed this was the most logical method to factor in the arbitrator's decision.

USPS attributes the reduced cost savings to the higher compensation employees receive in the POStPlan post offices under the post-arbitration decision staffing arrangements relative to the compensation these employees would have received under the original, pre-arbitration, staffing arrangements, as shown in fig. 6.

USPS officials told us that while the arbitration decision reduced the cost savings it expected to achieve, POStPlan was still the correct operational decision for USPS and its stakeholders.

LIMITATIONS AFFECT THE RELIABILITY OF USPS'S POSTPLAN COST-SAVINGS ESTIMATES AND THE ACCURACY OF ACTUAL SAVINGS ACHIEVED

USPS Estimates of Expected Cost Savings Have Limitations That Affect Reliability, Including Data Errors That Affect the Accuracy of Calculations of Actual Savings Achieved

We reviewed USPS's 2012 original POStPlan cost-savings estimate and 2015 estimate of the arbitration decision's impact on cost savings and found that while POStPlan most likely resulted in some cost savings, the estimates have limitations that affect their reliability. Specifically, the limitations include: (1) imprecise and incomplete labor costs, including errors in the underlying data that affect the accuracy of calculations of actual savings achieved; (2) lack of a sensitivity review; and (3) the exclusion of other factors that would be necessary to consider the net cost savings of the POStPlan initiative, particularly the potential impact of reduced hours on retail revenue.

Imprecise and Incomplete Labor Costs

Our guidance on assessing data reliability states that reliable data, which include estimates and projections, can be characterized as being accurate, valid, and complete.[33] For example, accurate data appropriately reflect the actual underlying information, valid data actually represent what is being measured, and complete data appropriately include all relevant information. Data should also be consistent, a subset of accuracy. Consistency can be impaired when there is an inconsistent interpretation of what data should be entered. Internal control standards adopted by USPS also state that program managers and decision makers need complete and accurate data to determine whether they are meeting their goals, and that they should use quality information to make informed decisions and evaluate an entity's performance in achieving key objectives and addressing risks.[34] These standards also note that the ability to generate quality information begins with the data used.

While USPS's original estimate of the savings it expected to achieve from POStPlan clearly states that it accounts for labor costs only, we found that the salary and benefits information that USPS used to calculate these labor costs was imprecise, and this imprecision contributes to inaccuracies in the estimate. For example:

- When calculating the "before POStPlan" labor costs, USPS used average postmaster salaries and benefits and, when calculating the "after POStPlan" costs, sometimes used the salary and benefits of newly hired postmasters and in other instances used the salary and benefits of incumbent postmasters. In a POStPlan advisory opinion, PRC noted that using an average postmaster salary is imprecise; that salaries at post offices vary, on average, by as much as $20,000 from the lowest to the highest salary; and that these variations can add up considerably when thousands of offices are considered.[35]
- Although USPS used average postmaster salaries and benefits for the "before POStPlan" labor costs, approximately 3,100 of the post offices included in the calculation were not being staffed by postmasters. These offices were being staffed by other types of employees, such as non-postmasters designated as "Officers in Charge," whose salaries were generally lower. In the POStPlan advisory opinion, PRC estimated that if it assumed salaries at these offices were at a level more representative of these other types of employees, the annual cost savings would be $386 million, not $516 million.

- In July 2012, USPS testified to PRC that about 60 percent of the postmasters at the would-be POStPlan post offices were eligible to retire, and therefore at the higher-end of their pay range. Relatedly, when calculating the "after POStPlan" labor costs at would-be Level 18 offices, USPS assumed that postmasters in those offices would receive the average Level 18 postmaster salary, rather than the minimum salary for that grade, a difference of as much as $25,000. In the POStPlan advisory opinion, PRC explained that this may have overstated these costs and estimated that if these assumptions were corrected, the annual cost savings would be $704 million, not $516 million.
- USPS included about 100 post offices that were actually closed or suspended in its calculation of labor costs despite stating that suspended offices were not part of POStPlan, that it would not re-visit closed offices' status, and that there were no plans to reopen these offices. In its POStPlan advisory opinion, PRC estimated that the cost savings would be $513 million, not $516 million, if USPS excluded these offices.

Similar to the original POStPlan cost-savings estimate, USPS's estimate of the arbitration decision's impact on cost savings has limitations related to imprecise labor costs, which, as noted above, contribute to inaccuracies. For example:

- USPS used a single, proxy employee category and hourly rate to represent all employees under the pre-arbitration POStPlan staffing arrangements, rather than the actual different rates these employees would have received, as described above. USPS used this proxy although it had the actual rates, and none of the actual rates matched the proxy rate.
- USPS included all Level 6 post offices and their associated positions' labor costs in its estimate. However, the arbitration decision did not affect the Level 6 PTPOs. This is inconsistent with how USPS treated Level 2 RMPOs in the estimate. These RMPOs were also not affected by the arbitration decision. Removing the Level 6 PTPOs from the estimate reduces the impact from about $181 million to about $170 million, meaning the revised savings would have been $348, not $337, million.

- USPS's post-arbitration decision estimate of $337 million in expected annual cost savings relies, in part, on USPS calculations of actual savings achieved due to POStPlan, but the accuracy of these actual savings calculations may be limited by errors in the underlying salaries and benefits data used to develop them. As described above, to arrive at $337 million, USPS subtracted the $181-million impact it calculated from the revised estimate of $518 million it developed in June 2015. Also as noted above, USPS developed that $518 million estimate in part by considering the actual savings it achieved from fiscal years 2012 to 2014. However, we found errors in USPS's salaries and benefits data that, according to USPS officials as of March 2016, may have been caused by employees' workhours being incorrectly recorded when employees worked in more than one office.[36] We found that these errors would result in some offices' salaries and benefits being understated, and others being overstated.[37] While understated and overstated costs at individual offices would likely offset each other in aggregate (i.e., when costs at all offices, either POStPlan or non-POStPlan, were considered), they do not offset when analyzing costs at just POStPlan post offices.[38] Given that according to USPS, its calculations of actual savings achieved consider costs at POStPlan—but not non-POStPlan— offices, the calculations may be limited by these errors. Additionally, according to USPS as of October 2015, thus far it has saved $306 million in labor costs from fiscal year 2012 to June 2015 as a result of POStPlan. Although POStPlan most likely resulted in cost savings because of the overall reduction in work hours at thousands of post offices, the accuracy of these calculated savings may also be limited by these errors.

USPS's calculation of labor costs in both its original and post-arbitration decision estimates was also incomplete. A full estimate of labor costs might have included additional labor cost elements. For example:

- USPS's original estimate did not include costs associated with the addition of supervisors at the Level 18 or above offices that remotely manage the POStPlan post offices due to their increased supervisory workload. Specifically, according to USPS officials, USPS added about 320 such positions, though not all as a result of POStPlan, and the average hourly pay for supervisors as of August 2015 was $48.73.[39]

- USPS's original estimate did not include one-time labor costs associated with separation incentives USPS offered to postmasters. According to USPS officials, acceptance of these separation incentives by POStPlan-affected postmasters cost USPS about $69 million.
- USPS's estimate of the arbitration decision's impact on cost savings excluded the potential cost impact of staffing changes in Level 18 post offices. Although USPS officials have stated that Level 18 offices are not part of POStPlan, the arbitration decision and a September 2014 memorandum of understanding that further implemented it required that a certain type of position staffing Level 18 offices be changed to a bargaining-unit clerk position.

No Sensitivity Analysis Conducted

Our cost-estimating best practices state that sensitivity analysis should generally be conducted when estimating costs, especially if changes in key assumptions would likely have a significant effect on the estimate.[40]

Sensitivity analyses identify a range of possible cost estimates by varying major assumptions, parameters, and inputs to enable an understanding of the impact altered assumptions have on estimated costs. This can also help managers and decisions makers identify risk areas and relevant program alternatives. Since uncertainty cannot be avoided, it is necessary to identify the elements that represent the most risk, which can be done through sensitivity analysis.

In developing its estimates, USPS did not conduct a sensitivity analysis to determine what would happen to estimated costs and savings should key assumptions it was making under POStPlan vary. For example, USPS officials told us that they recognized the possibility that APWU would challenge the planned staffing arrangements at POStPlan post offices. Despite this statement, in its original cost-savings estimate, USPS did not analyze the sensitivity of POStPlan labor costs to alternative staffing arrangements that might have been more in line with APWU's views on the staffing provisions specified in the USPS-APWU 2010-2015 CBA. USPS officials explained that they believed that savings associated with reduced hours at POStPlan post offices would significantly outweigh any reduction in savings should an arbitrator rule in APWU's favor. Similarly, USPS did not analyze the sensitivity of its estimated savings to possible changes in the benefits offered to USPS employees. For example, when calculating the salary and benefits of Postmaster Reliefs (PMR)—the employees expected to staff Level 2 and 4 RMPOs—USPS assumed that the only benefit they were eligible for was 1 hour of annual leave for every 20 hours worked.[41] However, in 2014, USPS began providing health coverage for PMRs who meet the requirements of the 2009 Affordable Care Act. Additionally, in both its estimates, USPS did not consider that staffing at offices may continue to change based on the workload reevaluations it plans to conduct. For example, under the original POStPlan staffing arrangements, a Level 4 RMPO staffed by a PMR earning $14.87 per hour could become a Level 6 RMPO staffed by a part-time postmaster earning $21.17 per hour if, after a re-evaluation of the office's workload, USPS determines that the office's workload has increased enough to justify a Level 6 classification. Thus, the number of offices at each level might continue to increase or decrease year after year. This also means that although USPS refers to its estimates as estimates of the "annual" savings it will achieve upon full POStPlan implementation, only a single-year estimate of savings can be produced at any given time, unless and until estimates of potential staffing changes in future years can be made.

Exclusion of Potential Impact on Revenue

OMB cost-estimating guidance states that agencies should determine whether an activity's benefits (savings) also take into account the costs incurred to implement it.[42] That is, the guidance suggests that it is the *net* benefit, or in this case, the *net* cost savings that should be considered. However, USPS's estimate did not include certain factors that could affect the net cost savings of the POStPlan initiative. In particular, USPS's original estimate did not include an analysis of the extent to which reduced hours at POStPlan post offices could affect revenue at those offices and across USPS. That is, it did not fully consider any offsetting financial losses that should be weighed against estimated savings.[43]

In July 2012, USPS testified to PRC that it did not anticipate losing revenue due to POStPlan, though it had not conducted a financial analysis to support this statement. Specifically, as described below, USPS expected any revenue lost at POStPlan post offices to be absorbed elsewhere. Despite this assumption, in its POStPlan advisory opinion, PRC stated that it was concerned that reduced retail hours may lead to reduced revenue and recommended that USPS undertake a post-implementation review of POStPlan to measure changes in revenue at POStPlan post offices. In September 2015, we asked USPS what, if any, steps it had taken to address PRC's recommendation. At that time, USPS had not yet taken steps to analyze changes in revenue at POStPlan post offices, though in January 2014—in response to a request from PRC— USPS submitted data to PRC on the fiscal year 2013 revenue earned in POStPlan post offices and in the Level 18 and above administrative post offices.[44] USPS officials told us that they planned to conduct a revenue analysis annually, comparing fiscal year over fiscal year, and later provided us with a preliminary analysis of changes from fiscal years 2014 to 2015.

USPS's preliminary POStPlan revenue analysis has limitations that may affect its representation of changes in revenue at POStPlan post offices and across USPS. This analysis showed that walk-in revenue declined by about 4 percent at POStPlan post offices, as well as at non-POStPlan offices, and at all offices in general. However, we found that USPS's calculation of revenue in POStPlan post offices was inconsistent with its definition of what constitutes POStPlan post offices. Specifically, USPS included revenue from the Level 18 or above administrative offices, though USPS does not define these as POStPlan post offices. Additionally, according to USPS officials, those are the offices most likely to absorb customers who are looking for nearby alternatives in the face of reduced hours at their local office. USPS also excluded the Level 6 PTPOs from its analysis although it considers these to be POStPlan post offices. After we inquired about the Level 6 PTPOs, USPS provided us with a revised analysis but, in this revision, USPS included the Level 18 and above administrative offices as POStPlan post offices. When we resorted the offices in USPS's analysis to exclude the Level 18 and above administrative offices from the "POStPlan post offices" category and include the Level 6 PTPOs in the "POStPlan post offices" category, we found that revenue declined by about 10 percent, not 4 percent in POStPlan post offices and by about 4 percent in non-POStPlan post offices.

To obtain a more comprehensive picture of how POStPlan may have affected revenue in the reduced-hour offices, we also analyzed the walk-in revenue earned at POStPlan post offices, by office level, for the most recent fiscal year (2015) compared to the most recent fiscal year in which no POStPlan implementation activities had begun to occur (2011).[45] We found that revenue at RMPOs in fiscal year 2015 was 29 percent lower than revenue, adjusted for inflation, in fiscal year 2011, with over a 50 percent decline in Level 2 RMPOs.[46] See table 1.

Table 1. Comparison of Revenue in U.S. Postal Service's (USPS) Post Office Structure Plan (POStPlan) Post Offices in Fiscal Years (FY) 2011 and 2015

POStPlan post office level	Adjusted revenue in FY 2011	Revenue in FY 2015	Change in revenue	Percentage decrease in revenue
Level 2 Remotely Managed Post Office (RMPO)	$24,022,163	$11,533,053	-$12,489,110	-52%
Level 4 RMPO	$245,991,620	$156,144,751	-$89,846,869	-37%
Level 6 RMPO	$294,996,354	$233,733,370	-$61,262,984	-21%
Total	$565,010,137	$401,411,174	-$163,598,963	-29%

Source: GAO analysis of data provided by USPS. | GAO-16-385

Notes: Numbers have been rounded to the nearest whole number and FY 2011 dollars were adjusted using the Gross Domestic Product deflator in order to be stated in 2015 dollars.

Some POStPlan post offices—including all Level 6 Part Time Post Offices—have been excluded from this analysis because USPS did not provide complete data for them. Because USPS completed POStPlan implementation during the third quarter of FY 2015 (i.e., in February 2015), information on revenue in FY 2015 cannot be considered completely as "after POStPlan implementation." Additionally, while this analysis helps to illustrate the potential effects of POStPlan on revenue, it does not fully measure it.

While our analysis shows that revenue at the POStPlan RMPOs declined by 29 percent, this revenue constituted a small portion of the total revenue from all of USPS's post offices. In January and February of 2016, USPS conducted additional analysis comparing fiscal years 2011 and 2015 post office walk-in revenue. According to this analysis, revenue from RMPOs in fiscal year 2011 accounted for just 4.5 percent of approximately $11.9 billion in total revenue earned from post offices that year and, in fiscal year 2015, 3.7 percent of approximately $10.8 billion in total revenue. Additionally, USPS's analysis showed that the Level 18 or above administrative offices experienced less of a decline in revenue than the RMPOs they remotely manage. Specifically, revenue at these offices in fiscal year 2011 was about $2.32 billion (adjusted for inflation) and, in fiscal year 2015, about $2.06 billion, a decline of about 11.2 percent. In its analysis, USPS also reported total revenue from all non-POStPlan offices. However, USPS's reported total again included the Level 6 PTPOs in this category. Overall, revenue at all post offices declined by about 14.6 percent from fiscal years 2011 to 2015 when fiscal year 2011 revenue is adjusted for inflation.

While both our and USPS's analyses comparing fiscal year 2011 and 2015, and USPS's analysis of changes from fiscal years 2014 to 2015 help to illustrate the potential effects of POStPlan on revenue, they do not fully measure it. In particular, analyzing the extent of revenue reductions that are independently due to POStPlan would require a more complex analysis that takes into account a variety of factors, and the USPS data available to us were not adequate to conduct such an analysis. For example, in addition to considering changes in revenue at POStPlan post offices by level, other factors need to also be considered, such as revenue changes in non-POStPlan offices and other retail channels within a reasonable distance to POStPlan offices, as well as at offices and channels not near POStPlan offices. Such an analysis would also need to consider other factors that may influence retail revenue over time. These factors could include, for example, the state of the general economy, the adoption of technology substitutes to traditional mail (such as e-mail, e-retail, and electronic bill payments), and relevant demographic characteristics that might affect mail volume, such as population density and household income. Such an analysis would also need to consider the movement of customer traffic to alternate ways of accessing postal services. For instance, in fiscal year 2015, about 46 percent of USPS's total retail revenue of about $19 billion was generated through these alternate access channels, which include usps.com, self-service kiosks, and third-party retail partners. In the case of POStPlan, USPS officials explained that since revenue from POStPlan post offices accounts for a small portion of total post office revenue and cost reductions due to POStPlan were expected to be much larger, cost savings due to POStPlan would likely outweigh lost revenue. However, analyzing the extent of revenue reductions that are independently due to POStPlan through a more complex analysis could be helpful in evaluating the overall impact of POStPlan if USPS expanded the initiative to additional post offices, as may occur due to the workload re-evaluations that USPS plans to conduct.

USPS Acknowledged the Limitations of Its Cost-Savings Estimates, Calculations of Actual Savings, and Revenue Analysis

Overall, USPS officials have acknowledged that their original POStPlan cost-savings estimate was not sophisticated—characterizing it as a rough estimate that used a "quick and dirty" approach—and have also acknowledged the limitations of their estimate of the arbitration decision's impact on cost savings. Prior to making any changes (like POStPlan) in the nature of postal services that are at least substantially nationwide in scope, USPS must request an advisory opinion from PRC on the change.[47] USPS officials explained that this process entails a review of the proposed initiative by PRC and that when making their case before PRC, USPS's legal counsel makes recommendations on strategy for the proceeding in consultation with other USPS staff. They further noted that in order to make an informed business decision prior to undertaking an initiative such as POStPlan, USPS undertakes reasonable efforts to appropriately assess the expected cost savings to determine whether the initiative is worth pursuing. The officials added that the nature and extent of this assessment varies by the specific circumstances, particularly, the financial circumstances facing USPS, the need for expedited implementation of an initiative, and USPS's overall confidence that an initiative will prudently reduce costs. USPS officials stated that in cases such as POStPlan, there is no strict guidance or thresholds that govern when cost-savings estimates should be rigorous versus when it is sufficient to use a less rigorous approach to gain a rough approximation, and there is no legal requirement to produce cost-savings estimates or to use a particular methodology. Instead, USPS officials said these are judgmental decisions.

Regarding USPS's calculations of actual savings achieved, USPS officials have also acknowledged the limitations of the underlying salaries and benefits data. For example, USPS officials acknowledged that the errors we found in these data would result in some offices' salaries and benefits being understated, and others being overstated. In February 2016, USPS officials told us that they were not previously aware of this issue and that they have begun to take steps to further understand the scope of the errors and how and why they occurred. As of March 14, 2016, USPS officials were continuing to assess this issue, but USPS's time frame for identifying the scope and resolving the issue remains unclear, and it is also unclear if USPS subsequently intends to update its calculations of actual savings achieved.

Regarding its analysis of changes in revenue from fiscal year 2014 to 2015, after reviewing our analysis of revenue at POStPlan post offices, USPS has also acknowledged that some PTPOs should have been included in its analysis and provided details on why it included these offices and the Level 18 and above administrative offices in the categories that it did. In particular, USPS officials told us that they agreed that some of the PTPOs should have been included in their analysis as POStPlan post offices and explained that they had included these offices in their analysis as non-POStPlan offices because this type of office existed prior to POStPlan. They also noted that they included the Level 18 and above administrative offices as POStPlan post offices because, as noted above, those would be the offices most likely to absorb customers who are looking for nearby alternatives in the face of reduced hours at their local post office. USPS officials also said that it is important to note that revenue declines at POStPlan post offices may not be fully lost to USPS because customers may use other nearby retail channels (e.g., the Level 18 or above offices, usps.com, etc.) instead. While we agree that ultimately, it is the revenue lost to USPS as a whole that is most relevant to USPS, it is still important to accurately represent the changes in revenue at the reduced-hour offices to fully understand the effects of POStPlan on these offices and the trade-offs necessary between costs and benefits, and to provide relevant information for program evaluation and future decision making.

CONCLUSION

We have long reported that USPS needs to restructure its operations to better reflect customers' changing use of the mail and to align its costs with revenues. Toward this end, USPS has proposed or started a number of initiatives, such as POStPlan, to increase efficiency and reduce costs as it seeks to improve its financial viability. Having reliable data and quality methods for calculating the potential savings USPS expects to achieve through these initiatives, the actual savings they achieve, and the potential effects they have on revenue are critical. Such rigor can help ensure that USPS officials and oversight bodies, such as PRC and Congress, have accurate and relevant information to help USPS strike the right balance between the costs and benefits of the various initiatives.

Although POStPlan was an initiative that affected about 66 percent of USPS's post offices and postmasters, USPS did not produce cost-savings estimates with the level of rigor that an initiative with such a large footprint may have warranted. Having reliable estimates of expected cost savings when initially making decisions could help ensure that USPS is achieving its goals, yet USPS's estimates of expected savings had limitations. For example, by not conducting a sensitivity analysis, as recommended by our cost-estimating guidance, USPS may have missed an opportunity to test how vulnerable its expected cost savings were to program changes. For instance, USPS may have been able to test how its expected savings would change should any of its assumptions change, as some later did because of the arbitration decision, which affected staffing arrangements at the majority of POStPlan post offices. If USPS had noticed significant differences in its projected labor costs and savings through a sensitivity analysis, it might have taken steps to address these vulnerabilities prior to announcing POStPlan. USPS believes that, given likely savings and the realities of postal operations, moving forward with POStPlan was the correct operational decision. However, for future initiatives like POStPlan, having guidance that clarifies when USPS should develop cost-savings estimates using a rigorous approach could help ensure that USPS produces estimates that thoroughly consider the scope of a program's implications, effects, and alternatives. Such an approach is particularly relevant given that USPS has projected unsustainable losses through fiscal year 2020 and beyond, may continue to develop efficiency and cost-savings initiatives, and will need quality information on the potential savings and effects associated with these initiatives.

Further, according to USPS as of October 2015, it has saved $306 million in labor costs from fiscal year 2012 to June 2015 as a result of POStPlan. While we recognize that POStPlan most likely resulted in some cost savings, the accuracy of USPS's calculation of savings may be limited by errors we found in USPS's salaries and benefits data, and thus, it is unclear whether USPS may have actually saved more or less. USPS's time frames for assessing and resolving this issue—and whether it intends to, subsequently, update its calculations of actual savings achieved—are also unclear. Finally, in its estimates of expected savings, USPS did not initially consider the effect that reduced retail hours may have on revenue and thus did not calculate an estimate of *net* cost savings. This means USPS had an incomplete picture of the effects of POStPlan. Even the preliminary analysis of changes in revenue that USPS later conducted was limited because it was not consistent with USPS's definition of what constitutes POStPlan post offices. Improving the quality of future POStPlan revenue analyses, especially as the program potentially expands to additional offices, could help USPS better understand the implications of POStPlan and inform future decision-making as USPS conducts workload re-evaluations of post offices.

Recommendations for Executive Action

The Postmaster General should direct executive leaders to:

- establish guidance that clarifies when USPS should develop cost-savings estimates using a rigorous approach that includes, for example, a sensitivity analysis and consideration of other factors that could affect net costs and savings, versus when it is sufficient to develop a rough estimate;
- continue to take steps to assess and resolve the salaries and benefits data errors and, subsequently, update calculations of actual cost savings achieved due to POStPlan as appropriate;
- and verify that calculations of changes in revenue at POStPlan post offices in USPS's revenue analyses are consistent with USPS's definition of POStPlan post offices and take steps to consider when it may be appropriate to develop an approach for these analyses that will allow USPS to more fully consider the effects of POStPlan on retail revenue across USPS.

Agency Comments and Our Evaluation

We provided a draft of this report to PRC and USPS for their review and comment. PRC provided comments in an e-mail and stated that it found the report accurately reflects PRC's advisory opinion and actions regarding POStPlan. USPS provided a written response. In the written response, USPS disagreed with the overall tone and title of our report, provided observations on our recommendations but did not state whether it agreed or disagreed with them, and disagreed with some of the specific examples we use in our report.

Regarding the tone and title of our report, in its response USPS reported that it does not see a basis for any conclusion other than that, with POStPlan, it is saving substantial amounts from the reduction in work hours and the use of lower cost labor. It further stated that POStPlan was a reasonable initiative in light of declining mail transactions and the need to right-size its infrastructure to support the retail needs of the country. Finally, USPS said that it believes POStPlan was and remains a prudent business decision. Our report does not comment directly on the reasonableness of the POStPlan initiative or whether it was a prudent business decision, but we note in our report that USPS believed POStPlan was a proper operational decision for USPS and its stakeholders. Instead, our report focuses on USPS's estimates of savings due to POStPlan. We do not disagree that POStPlan most likely resulted in some savings due to reduced work hours and have clarified our report to state such. However, as we mention in the report, USPS's calculations of the actual savings achieved may be limited by errors in USPS's salaries and benefits data, and thus, USPS may have understated or overstated the amount it has saved. We also revised the title of the report in response to USPS's concern.

Regarding our first recommendation that USPS establish guidance that clarifies when USPS should develop cost-savings estimates using a rigorous approach versus when it is sufficient to develop a rough estimate, USPS said that it performed the level of analysis necessary to support the decision to move forward with POStPlan and that there is not a concrete set of business rules that determine the level of analysis that should be conducted. Instead, USPS noted that its management intends to be guided by a variety of factors, on a case-by-case basis. These factors include: (1) the cost associated with the development of rigorous financial information, (2) whether savings are the sole factor motivating the decision, and (3) the amount of time that must be committed to performing detailed analysis, among other things. USPS added that decisions based on more complex operational changes and risk may require more detailed analysis. While we appreciate that there is value to considering the types of analyses to perform on a case-by-case basis, the factors that USPS lists in its written response are precisely the type of factors that could be included (or expanded upon) in guidance that clarifies how to make those case-by-case decisions. Additionally, as we note in our report, we believe such guidance will be helpful to USPS and its oversight bodies as it considers future initiatives. As such, we continue to believe our recommendation is appropriate.

Regarding our second recommendation that USPS continue to assess and resolve errors in its salaries and benefits data and, as appropriate, update its calculations of actual savings achieved due to POStPlan, USPS said that it did not rely on this type of data in its original estimate of expected cost savings. We recognize that USPS did not rely on these data in that estimate. Instead, our report mentions that such data affected USPS's post-arbitration decision estimate of expected savings and were used to calculate actual savings achieved thus far. Regarding the latter, USPS noted in its written response that due to system limitations, it cannot change past, existing data, but that it will continue to identify and rectify the causes of the data anomalies. USPS also noted that as more detailed information may be necessary in the future, it is reviewing possible future system or process improvement opportunities. These are positive steps to ensure that USPS is addressing these data issues and reviewing opportunities for future improvements.

Regarding our third recommendation that USPS (1) verify that calculations of changes in revenue at POStPlan post offices in its revenue analyses are consistent with USPS's definition of POStPlan post offices and (2) take steps to consider when it may be appropriate to develop an approach that more fully considers the effects of POStPlan on revenue across USPS, USPS did not directly address either part of this recommendation. Instead, USPS provided information on revenue at POStPlan post offices in 2011 and 2015 (such as the portion of total walk-in revenue these offices constituted), much of which is included in our report. USPS also re-iterated that it expected revenue would shift from POStPlan post offices to the Level 18 and above offices that remotely manage the POStPlan offices, and noted that USPS's revenue analysis supports that assumption. The intent of our recommendation was not to disagree with this assumption. Rather, the intent of our recommendation is to help ensure that USPS and its oversight bodies have quality information on the changes in revenue at POStPlan post offices in order to fully understand the effects of POStPlan. Key to having such information is ensuring that the calculations of changes in revenue are consistent with USPS's definition of what constitutes a "POStPlan post office." As such, we continue to believe that verifying the accuracy of its calculations is important. Additionally, our report acknowledges the small portion of total walk-in revenue that POStPlan post offices constitute, and notes that a more complex analysis could be helpful if USPS expanded the initiative to additional offices, as may occur due to the workload reevaluations that USPS plans to conduct. We therefore continue to believe that USPS should take steps to consider at what point such an analysis may be warranted.

Finally, USPS disagreed with some of the specific examples we use in our report. In particular:

- USPS disagreed with an example showing that its original cost-savings estimate was incomplete due to the omission of costs associated with separation incentives offered to postmasters, noting that "annualized savings" estimates are generally not reduced by such start-up costs. We do not disagree that annualized savings are one way to measure cost savings. However, as we note in our report, OMB cost-estimating guidance states that agencies should also take into account the costs incurred to implement an activity, suggesting that it is the net cost savings that should be considered. As such, a fully complete cost-savings estimate would consider such start-up costs. Similarly, USPS disagreed in another instance that showed the saved salary USPS authorized to postmasters contributed to the incompleteness of its original estimate and noted that these salary payments were not planned at the inception of the program. We have updated our report to reflect that these payments were not planned.

- Finally, USPS disagreed with statements showing that the change made to staffing in Level 18 post offices as a result of the POSPlan arbitration decision is tied to POStPlan, noting that this change was related to a separate grievance and that this separate grievance was specifically identified in a footnote in the POStPlan arbitration decision. We do not disagree with the idea that this change was a resolution of a separate grievance and that the footnote USPS refers to cites this separate grievance. However, we disagree that the change was not at all tied to POStPlan. The connection to POStPlan is clear in the arbitration decision's wording. Specifically, in the arbitration decision, the arbitrator ruled that Level 4 RMPOs should be staffed by PSEs. When stating its ruling regarding the staffing change in Level 18 offices, the arbitration decision clearly states, "In view of the increased use of PSEs in Level 4 RMPOs .... I further order that all Level 18 post offices that are currently staffed by PSEs with the designation code 81-8 will now be staffed with a career employee." Therefore, it is clear that changes in staffing at Level 4 RMPOs (which were part of POStPlan) also affected the resolution of this separate dispute.

Lori Rectanus
Director
Physical Infrastructure Issues

APPENDIX I: OBJECTIVES, SCOPE, AND METHODOLOGY

This report examines (1) the actions the U.S. Postal Service (USPS) took to implement the Post Office Structure Plan (POStPlan) before the September 2014 arbitration decision and the savings USPS estimated POStPlan would achieve, (2) the effect USPS determined the arbitration decision had on

POStPlan staffing and cost savings, and (3) whether USPS's POStPlan cost-savings estimates are reliable and any limitations of the estimates.

To describe the POStPlan initiative, determine the actions USPS took to implement it before the September 2014 arbitration decision and identify the effects USPS determined the decision had on POStPlan staffing, we reviewed relevant laws, regulations, documentation and data, and conducted interviews. Specifically, we reviewed USPS guidance, policies, procedures, and other documents related to POStPlan planning and implementation, such as fact sheets, employee notification letters, and information submitted during the Postal Regulatory Commission's (PRC) 2012 POStPlan proceeding. We reviewed USPS's 2014 and 2015 annual reports to Congress and *2013 Five-Year Business Plan.*[1] We also reviewed documentation related to the arbitration in particular, such as the arbitration decision,[2] subsequent memorandums of understanding between USPS and the American Postal Workers Union (APWU) that further implemented the decision, and the 2010-2015 collective bargaining agreement between USPS and APWU. We obtained written responses and data from USPS officials on the arbitration decision and POStPlan implementation from 2012 to 2015, such as data on the number of post offices where USPS reduced hours from 2012 to 2015 and postmasters affected by POStPlan. We assessed the reliability of these data by comparing them to other information obtained from USPS and asking USPS questions about data sources, quality, and timeliness. We found these data reliable for the purpose of describing the progress and status of POStPlan before and after the arbitration decision. We also reviewed prior GAO reports and documentation from USPS stakeholders, including PRC and USPS's two postmaster associations—the National Association of Postmasters of the United States (NAPUS) and the National League of Postmasters of the United States (NLPM). For example, we reviewed PRC's advisory opinion on POStPlan and the transcript of PRC's POStPlan hearing, which it held on July 11, 2012.[3] We selected NAPUS and NLPM due to their role as management associations that USPS must consult with and because they represent POStPlan-affected postmasters. We selected PRC due its oversight role over USPS. We interviewed USPS officials and NAPUS, NLPM, and PRC officials to obtain additional information, views, and context on POStPlan. We also contacted APWU, but APWU officials did not accept our invitation for a meeting.

To determine the cost savings USPS originally estimated it would achieve through POStPlan, the effect it estimated the arbitration decision had on savings, and the reliability and limitations of these estimates, we reviewed

USPS's POStPlan cost-savings estimates and compared the estimates to relevant criteria. Specifically, we reviewed USPS's 2012 estimate of the savings it expected to achieve through POStPlan and its 2015 estimate of the arbitration decision's impact on expected cost savings. We obtained USPS documentation and written responses related to POStPlan cost savings, interviewed USPS officials, and obtained documentation and interviewed officials from NAPUS, NLPM, and PRC to determine how USPS developed its estimates, the assumptions it used, the potential sources of uncertainty, the types of inputs included and omitted, and these stakeholders' views. We then assessed the reliability and soundness of these estimates using guidance on assessing the reliability of data (which are defined as including estimates—such as estimates of cost savings—and projections),[4] cost estimating guidance,[5] and internal controls standards adopted by USPS to determine the extent to which the estimates comported with these criteria.[6] We reviewed these standards and guidance and then selected those practices that, in our professional judgment, were most applicable given that POStPlan is an efficiency and cost-savings initiative and given USPS's financial condition. In particular, we assessed the estimates' accuracy, validity, completeness, and consistency; any use of sensitivity analyses; and consideration of net cost-savings factors. We discuss the limitations of the estimates in this report. We also obtained USPS data on actual cost savings achieved from fiscal year 2012 to June 2015 (the most recent data available at the time of our review) due to POStPlan, and hourly pay rates in POStPlan post offices under the pre- and post-arbitration decision POStPlan staffing arrangements. We assessed the reliability of these data by comparing them to other information obtained from USPS and asking USPS officials questions about data sources, quality, and timeliness, and, for the actual savings data, reviewing how consistently USPS's data files followed the methodology USPS officials described to us. Regarding the actual savings data, we found that USPS's data files when USPS first began tracking savings did not always follow the methodology USPS described to us. While USPS officials did not provide explanations for these inconsistencies, USPS updated its methodology for tracking POStPlan cost savings beginning in fiscal year 2015. However, we also found errors in the salaries and benefits data USPS used to calculate actual savings achieved; we discuss the limitations in this report. Regarding the hourly pay-rate data, we found these data reliable for the purpose of describing hourly pay rates in POStPlan post offices according to USPS. It was beyond the scope of our review to assess whether POStPlan was a prudent business decision.

Finally, to better understand the potential effects of POStPlan and the arbitration decision, we analyzed (1) salaries and benefits paid, and (2) the walk-in revenue earned at POStPlan post offices, by post office level, for periods before and after POStPlan implementation.[7] We used data provided by USPS, as follows:

- **Salaries and benefits data**: USPS provided us data on the salaries and benefits it paid to POStPlan employees[8] in POStPlan post offices in the third quarter of fiscal year 2011 (i.e., April, May, and June 2011). According to USPS officials, these data represented all salaries and benefits paid to all relevant employees during that period.[9] USPS provided us the same information for the third quarter of fiscal year 2015.[10] To make the fiscal year 2011 data comparable to the fiscal year 2015 data, we adjusted the fiscal year 2011 salaries and benefits using adjustment factors provided by USPS officials.[11]
- **Revenue data**: USPS provided us data on the revenue in POStPlan post offices in fiscal years 2011 and 2015. We adjusted fiscal year 2011 dollars using the Gross Domestic Product deflator so that they would be stated in 2015 dollars.
- **Office level classification data**: USPS provided us data on what level each POStPlan post office is classified as of October 2015 (i.e., whether it is a Level 2, 4, or 6 remotely managed post office (RMPO) or part time post office (PTPO)).

Although USPS officials stated that these data provided included all POStPlan post offices, we found that they did not always include information for the same set of offices, and when providing these data, USPS officials did not provide explanations for why the number of POStPlan post offices differed. As such, regarding our revenue analysis, we excluded offices as necessary in order to have as complete a set of information as possible for as many offices as possible with what was provided. Specifically, of those offices for which we had level information, we excluded those for which we did not have revenue data for both periods. In particular, USPS's data did not include complete information on revenue in both periods at the majority of the about 400 Level 6 PTPOs. Thus, we excluded the Level 6 PTPOs from our results. We also excluded one Level 6 RMPO for this reason. Additionally, we excluded four offices that had multiple level classifications. Of those four, three were classified as both Levels 4 and 18, and one was classified as both Levels 6 and 18. Despite these exclusions, we found these data reliable for the purpose of describing changes in revenue at POStPlan post offices. Regarding our salaries and benefits analysis, in analyzing USPS's salaries and benefits data, we found that these data were not reliable due to errors in how USPS recorded the hours its employees worked.

End Notes

[1] This amount includes USPS's outstanding debt ($15 billion); and unfunded liabilities for retiree health benefits ($54.8 billion), pensions ($24.1 billion), workers' compensation ($18.8 billion); and other miscellaneous liabilities ($12.5 billion). It does not include assets including cash and noncurrent assets largely comprising property and equipment measured at historic purchase value after depreciation, which totaled $24 billion in fiscal year 2015.

[2] 39 U.S.C. § 2005(a). USPS reached its statutory borrowing limit of $15 billion in 2012.

[3] GAO, *High-Risk Series: Restructuring the U.S. Postal Service to Achieve Sustainable Financial Viability*, GAO-09-937SP (Washington, D.C.: July 2009); *High-Risk Series: An Update*, GAO-11-278 (Washington, D.C.: February 2011); *High-Risk Series: An Update*, GAO-13-283 (Washington, D.C.: February 2013); and *High-Risk Series: An Update*, GAO-15-290 (Washington, D.C.: February 2015).

[4] 39 U.S.C. § 101(a).

[5] For example, USPS announced plans to reduce the network's footprint and introduce retail alternatives in 2002; introduced an initiative in 2009 that resulted in the closure of 131 facilities; and, in 2011, announced an initiative (which it ultimately did not implement) that would have evaluated almost 3,700 post offices for possible closure.

[6] PRC is an independent establishment of the executive branch that has regulatory oversight over USPS.

[7] American Postal Workers Union, AFL-CIO and U.S. Postal Service, No. Q11C-4Q-C 12243899 (Goldberg, 2014).

[8] PRC, *Advisory Opinion on Post Office Structure Plan*, Docket No. N2012-2 (Washington, D.C.: Aug. 23, 2012), accessed April 2016, http://www.prc.gov/dockets/doclist/N2012-2/Advisory-Opinion/. Prior to making any changes (like POStPlan) in the nature of postal services that are at least substantially nationwide in scope, USPS must request an advisory opinion from PRC. 39 U.S.C. § 3661(b), as implemented by 39 C.F.R. § 3001. 71 et seq.

[9] APWU represents clerks, maintenance employees, motor vehicle operators, and nonmail-processing professional employees.

[10] GAO, *Assessing the Reliability of Computer-Processed Data*, GAO-09-680G (Washington, D.C.: July 2009).

[11] GAO, *Cost Estimating and Assessment Guide: Best Practices for Developing and Managing Capital Program Costs*, GAO-09-3SP (Washington, D.C.: March 2009). We did not assess USPS's estimates against all of the standards in this cost-estimating guidance because some overlapped with our data reliability guidance and, thus, were duplicative, and others were not applicable to non-capital programs. Instead, we focused on sensitivity analysis because the guidance emphasizes that sensitivity analysis is a best practice in all estimates of costs. OMB, *Circular A-94: Guidelines and Discount Rates for Benefit-Cost Analysis of Federal Programs* (Washington, D.C.: Oct. 29, 1992). We found OMB's cost-estimating guidance applicable because it contains tenets that are consistent with the management practices of

leading organizations and is intended to help agencies ensure that the benefits of a program or activity are greater than the costs incurred to implement it.

[12] Committee of Sponsoring Organizations of the Treadway Commission (COSO*), Internal Control—Integrated Framework* (2013).

[13] Walk-in revenue is revenue earned at post office retail counters, including revenue from USPS's mobile point of sale devices.

[14] In addition to revenue from post offices, total retail revenue includes revenue from alternate access channels, such as usps.com; self-service kiosks; non-USPS-operated postal facilities, such as Contract Postal Units; and USPS approved shippers and stamp retailers. USPS's total, overall, revenue in fiscal year 2015 was about $69 billion.

[15] The personnel-related costs included in USPS's financial reports include compensation and benefits, workers' compensation, and retiree health-benefit premiums, which include the legally mandated prefunding of retiree health benefits.

[16] Postal Support Employees are employees hired by USPS for a period not to exceed 360 days (eligible for renewal).

[17] Effective November 1, 2016, NAPUS and NLPM will merge into a single postmaster association known as the United Postmasters and Managers of America.

[18] 39 U.S.C. § 1004(b).

[19] Prior to POStPlan, USPS had announced the Retail Access Optimization Initiative in July 2011, which could have resulted in the closure of almost 3,700 post offices. However, some postal stakeholders—such as PRC, NAPUS, NLPM, and some Members of Congress—expressed concerns with this initiative. USPS ultimately did not implement it, and POStPlan reflected a determination by USPS to explore options to adjust its retail service without closing offices.

[20] Specifically, USPS analyzed workload data from fiscal year 2011 at certain offices that according to USPS, were selected because the level of retail activity at the offices indicated that they could continue to serve customer needs with reduced retail hours. USPS did not analyze the other 8,975 post offices as part of POStPlan. In USPS's analysis, the daily workload represented the sum total of employee hours spent performing mail and post office box distribution, retail sales, and administrative functions, such as personnel and time and attendance work.

[21] USPS classifies non-reduced-hour offices into numerical levels based on a system that links the responsibilities and workload at each office to the salary of its postmaster. Prior to POStPlan, there were already 4,100 Level 18 offices. These 4,100 offices were originally part of the 8,975 offices that USPS did not analyze as part of POStPlan.

[22] In addition to Level 18, non-reduced-hour post offices may also be Levels 19, 20, 21, 22, 23, 24, 25, or 26.

[23] Generally, USPS decided that offices further than 25 miles from a neighboring office would be considered especially isolated.

[24] USPS conducts these non-POStPlan reviews when the postmaster position at an office becomes vacant, when the postmaster of an office believes the office's revenue or workload has increased or decreased to such a degree that a review is warranted, or at least once every 3 years.

[25] USPS's field structure consists of area and district offices. Each district office reports to a designated area office, which, in turn, reports to USPS headquarters.

[26] According to USPS POStPlan planning documentation, USPS sent the survey to all addresses serviced by the post offices under consideration, and customers could also request surveys at the post office's retail counter.

[27] Between September 2014 and February 2015, USPS completed reducing hours at approximately 3,600 POStPlan post offices and—although USPS officials consider POStPlan fully implemented as of February 2015—at 1 additional office in May 2015. According to USPS data as of August 17, 2015, there are 1,836 Level 2 RMPOs, 6,671 Level 4 RMPOs, 3,882 Level 6 RMPOs, and 406 Level 6 PTPOs. As of this same date, there are 8,599 Level 18 offices. These numbers differ from those originally announced in May 2012 because, based on re-evaluations of workload at POStPlan and Level 18 post offices that USPS conducted throughout POStPlan implementation, some offices' hours—and thus Level—have increased or decreased. USPS has put additional re-evaluations on hold and would not implement additional changes until fiscal year 2017.

[28] Of the about 4,100 that separated, about 2,800 did so through the May 2012 incentive offer and the remaining approximately 1,300 did so through other means, such as employee death, removal, disability retirement, or transfer to another federal agency.

[29] Additional POStPlan-affected postmasters that had not separated or been reassigned prior to the decision did so by the February 2015 deadline. Specifically, about 1,900 separated and about 1,500 were reassigned. Of the about 1,900 who separated, about 1,400 did so through the July 2014 incentive offer (which became effective September 30, 2014), about 450 did so through the RIF, and the remainder did so through the other means described above.

[30] Specifically, the arbitrator ruled that staffing under POStPlan violated the following two provisions of the CBA: (1) each newly created or revised position that contains non-managerial and non-supervisory duties shall be assigned to the most appropriate craft unit and (2) when non-managerial or non-supervisory work which was being performed by supervisors is no longer performed by supervisors, it must be assigned to clerk craft employees.

[31] Regarding Level 2 RMPOs, the arbitrator noted that the majority of employees in Level 2 RMPOs never performed any supervisory work. The staffing of PTPOs was not at issue in the filed grievance.

[32] Work rules are the rules governing an employee's wages, hours, and working conditions and how USPS can deploy its employees. Work rules are often incorporated into CBAs as contract provisions. For example, these provisions specify such things as who is assigned to perform overtime work.

[33] GAO-09-680G.

[34] COSO, *Internal Control—Integrated Framework.*

[35] PRC, *Advisory Opinion on Post Office Structure Plan.*

[36] We realized these errors as we attempted to analyze salaries and benefits paid in POStPlan post offices, by office level, for a period before and after POStPlan implementation using data provided by USPS. See appendix I for detail regarding these data. In analyzing these data, we found that some offices were recorded as having paid a negative amount in salaries and benefits to certain categories of employees, and some offices were recorded as having paid a negative amount office-wide when combining these employee categories. USPS officials explained that they believe these negative amounts were due to the use of incorrect employee category codes during the manual recording of workhour transfers from one office to another—that is, when an employee that normally works at one office works some hours at different offices. Because the use of an incorrect employee code could be accounting for costs at an incorrect labor rate, the labor costs at both the office that "borrowed" the employee and the office that "lent" the employee could be incorrect. USPS officials acknowledged that a significant amount of this borrowing and lending of employees across offices occurs, and thus it is possible that additional errors exist but were

not noticeable because the amounts, while understated or overstated, did not appear as negative. While the original analysis through which we encountered this error included fiscal year 2011 and 2015 data, we subsequently also found similar errors in the fiscal year 2012 to 2014 data used in USPS's calculations of actual POStPlan cost savings achieved.

[37] Despite these recording errors, USPS officials told us that all employees were paid the correct amounts.

[38] This is the case because, according to USPS officials, it is possible the employee transfers may have occurred among both POStPlan and non-POStPlan offices. Understated and overstated costs at individual offices also do not offset when analyzing costs by office level since, according to USPS officials, these transfers occurred among offices of different levels.

[39] Similarly, USPS's original estimate did not include payments associated with "saved salary" offers USPS made to employees. Specifically, USPS allowed some POStPlanaffected postmasters who accepted demotions to keep their pre-POStPlan salaries and benefits, rather than downgrading their pay according to the new POStPlan staffing arrangements. According to USPS officials, it authorized saved salary for about 1,000 employees during POStPlan implementation; as of August 5, 2015, 656 employees continue to receive it, and saved salary is authorized until the end of fiscal year 2016. However, USPS told us that these salary payments were not included because they were not planned at the inception of the POStPlan initiative.

[40] GAO-09-3SP.

[41] PMRs are employees who serve as a relief or leave replacement during the absence of a postmaster in certain post offices.

[42] OMB, *Circular A-94.*

[43] USPS's estimate also did not include the one-time costs associated with community outreach and building modifications. As previously described, USPS surveyed and held meetings in POStPlan-affected communities during POStPlan implementation. According to USPS officials, USPS spent about $389,200 on costs associated with this outreach. USPS also made building modifications to some POStPlan post offices to maintain customers' access to their mail receptacles. USPS officials told us that as of August 5, 2015, USPS has made modifications to about 4,400 offices and spent about $8 million on the modifications to about half of those offices. USPS did not provide an estimate of what it cost to modify the remaining half.

[44] PRC requested these data as part of its fiscal year 2013 annual compliance review, which is a review process that PRC conducts annually to determine whether the rates and services USPS offered during the subject fiscal year comply with applicable legal requirements. This process results in the issuance of an Annual Compliance Determination by PRC.

[45] See appendix I for detail regarding the methodology of this analysis.

[46] Fiscal year 2011 dollars were adjusted using the Gross Domestic Product deflator in order to be stated in 2015 dollars. These results exclude Level 6 PTPOs because USPS's data did not include complete information on revenue in both periods at the majority of Level 6 PTPOs.

[47] 39 U.S.C. § 3661(b), as implemented by 39 C.F.R. § 3001. 71 et seq.

End Notes for Appendix I

[1] USPS, *2014 Annual Report to Congress* (Washington, D.C.: 2014); *2015 Annual Report to Congress* (Washington, D.C.: 2015); and *2013 Five-Year Business Plan* (Washington, D.C.: Apr. 16, 2013).

[2] American Postal Workers Union, AFL-CIO and U.S. Postal Service, No. Q11C-4Q-C 12243899 (Goldberg, 2014).

[3] PRC, *Advisory Opinion on Post Office Structure Plan*, Docket No. N2012-2 (Washington, D.C.: Aug. 23, 2012); *Official Transcript of Proceedings Before the Postal Regulatory Commission, In the Matter of: Post Office Structure Plan*, Docket No. N2012-2 (Washington, D.C.: July 11, 2012).

[4] GAO, *Assessing the Reliability of Computer-Processed Data*, GAO-09-680G (Washington, D.C.: July 2009).

[5] GAO, *Cost Estimating and Assessment Guide: Best Practices for Developing and Managing Capital Program Costs*, GAO-09-3SP (Washington, D.C.: March 2009). We did not assess USPS's estimates against all of the standards in this cost-estimating guidance because some overlapped with our data reliability guidance and, thus, were duplicative, and others were not applicable to non-capital programs. Instead, we focused on sensitivity analysis because the guidance emphasizes that sensitivity analysis is a best practice in all estimates of costs. Office of Management and Budget (OMB), Circular A-94, *Guidelines and Discount Rates for Benefit-Cost Analysis of Federal Programs* (Washington, D.C.: Oct. 29, 1992). We found OMB's cost-estimating guidance applicable because it contains tenets that are consistent with the management practices of leading organizations and is intended to help agencies ensure that the benefits of a program or activity are greater than the costs incurred to implement it.

[6] Committee of Sponsoring Organizations of the Treadway Commission (COSO*), Internal Control—Integrated Framework* (2013).

[7] Walk-in revenue is revenue earned at post office retail counters, including revenue from USPS's mobile point of sale devices.

[8] We use the term "POStPlan employees" to refer to specific types of employees within USPS that staff POStPlan post offices. Generally, these employees include postmasters, postmaster reliefs, certain types of clerks, and postal support employees. The data USPS provided tracked total salaries and benefits paid by certain employee categories that, according to USPS officials, capture all relevant POStPlan employees.

[9] According to USPS officials, the salaries and benefits paid include all pay, including overtime and leave pay.

[10] These data represent the same pay periods. We used data from before and after POStPlan implementation. USPS defines implementation as when it reduced an office's hours; USPS completed POStPlan implementation in February 2015. Thus, we used data on the third quarter of fiscal year 2015 because it was the first quarter after USPS completed POStPlan implementation, and the most recent data available at the time USPS provided the information. We used data on the third quarter of fiscal year 2011 in order to ensure the quarters we were comparing were identical and to ensure we captured a point in time in which no POStPlan implementation activities had begun to occur. While USPS did not begin reducing hours at POStPlan post offices until the first quarter of fiscal year 2013, implementation activities began prior to this time. For example, USPS offered a separation incentive to postmasters in the third quarter of 2012.

[11] Specifically, USPS provided us with the cost-of-living adjustment increases, step and general increases, and raises that employees in each category would have received through fiscal year 2015.

INDEX

A

access, 5, 18, 34, 75, 116, 129, 141, 143
accounting, 19, 76, 90, 100, 111, 142
adjustment, 13, 139, 144
agencies, 93, 94, 95, 126, 135, 141, 144
Alaska, 23, 45, 46
American Postal Workers Union (APWU), 18, 28, 29, 30, 31, 58, 59, 71, 75, 78, 82, 100, 107, 109, 112, 113, 115, 118, 125, 137, 140, 144
amortization, 100
appropriations, vii, 4, 50, 85, 86, 87, 99
Appropriations Act, 51
arbitration, 28, 30, 105, 106, 107, 109, 115, 118, 119, 120, 121, 123, 124, 125, 130, 132, 134, 136, 137, 139
assessment, 96, 130
assets, 6, 16, 18, 29, 52, 55, 58, 59, 60, 75, 82, 83, 100, 101, 103, 140
audit(s), 79, 94, 110
authority(ies), 5, 21, 22, 34, 35, 37, 55, 82, 98, 108, 115
automation, 73

B

background information, vii, 1
banking, 2, 7, 33, 34, 36, 37, 61, 62
banks, 35, 37, 62
bargaining, 71, 72, 73, 80, 99, 104, 106, 107, 113, 118, 119, 125, 137
benefits, 1, 3, 15, 16, 17, 19, 36, 46, 49, 54, 55, 58, 62, 66, 68, 71, 76, 80, 81, 82, 83, 86, 87, 88, 89, 90, 91, 92, 93, 94, 95, 96, 97, 98, 100, 101, 102, 103, 104, 107, 110, 112, 117, 120, 122, 124, 126, 130, 131, 132, 133, 134, 138, 139, 140, 141, 142, 143, 144
breakdown, 15

C

Cabinet, 2, 3
capital programs, 140, 144
cash, 5, 6, 52, 54, 86, 89, 90, 91, 100, 140
category a, 40, 82, 123, 127
challenges, vii, 1, 2, 3, 14, 15, 31, 53, 59, 74, 101
classification, 60, 126, 139
closure, 2, 18, 21, 24, 26, 43, 47, 49, 50, 57, 140, 141
collective bargaining, 98, 104, 107, 112, 137
collective bargaining agreement (CBA), 99, 107, 112, 115, 118, 125, 137, 142
Committee of Sponsoring Organizations of the Treadway Commission (COSO), 108, 141, 142, 144
communities, 26, 48, 115, 143

compensation, 14, 15, 16, 20, 30, 54, 55, 76, 77, 83, 90, 103, 121, 140, 141
Competitive Products, 1, 7, 53
complexity, 62
compliance, 143
composition, 30, 65, 66, 96, 112
Congress, v, vii, 1, 2, 3, 4, 16, 17, 21, 22, 27, 31, 34, 37, 50, 51, 54, 55, 59, 60, 61, 62, 63, 67, 69, 70, 73, 74, 82, 85, 86, 88, 89, 91, 92, 97, 99, 100, 101, 102, 103, 131, 137, 141, 143
consolidation, 2, 14, 21, 24, 26, 82
Consumer Price Index (CPI), 12
cost, 4, 17, 18, 20, 26, 30, 31, 32, 52, 60, 62, 65, 74, 75, 76, 77, 83, 86, 87, 93, 94, 95, 96, 98, 101, 102, 105, 106, 107, 109, 117, 119, 120, 121, 122, 123, 124, 125, 126, 129, 130, 131, 132, 133, 134, 135, 137, 140, 143, 144
cost savings, 20, 105, 106, 107, 109, 117, 119, 121, 122, 123, 124, 125, 126, 129, 130, 131, 132, 133, 134, 135, 137, 143
customers, 17, 21, 26, 31, 33, 113, 115, 116, 127, 131, 141, 143

D

decision makers, 107, 122
deflator, 128, 139, 143
demographic characteristics, 129
Denmark, 61
Department of Labor (DOL), 6
Department of the Treasury, 51, 52
depository institutions, 37, 63
deposits, 7, 35
depreciation, 16, 140
disability, 97, 142
distribution, 14, 56, 141
draft, 133

E

early retirement, 97
employees, 14, 15, 16, 17, 18, 19, 20, 25, 26, 28, 29, 30, 31, 49, 54, 55, 58, 65, 66, 67, 68, 69, 70, 71, 73, 74, 75, 76, 77, 78, 79, 80, 81, 82, 83, 86, 87, 88, 89, 90, 92, 93, 94, 95, 96, 97, 98, 99, 100, 101, 102, 103, 104, 106, 109, 111, 112, 114, 115, 117, 118, 119, 120, 121, 122, 123, 124, 126, 139, 140, 141, 142, 143, 144
employment, 15, 29, 30, 68, 70, 71, 73, 78, 79, 82, 84
enforcement, 103
enrollment, 41, 42
equipment, 26, 140
Evaluated Postmaster (EPM), 33, 108
executive branch, 2, 3, 74, 86, 140
expenditures, 15

F

FDIC, 36, 62
federal agency, 86, 89, 142
federal government, 86, 93, 94, 95, 98, 99, 103
federal law, 103
Federal Register, 53
federal workforce, 95, 96
financial, vii, 1, 2, 3, 4, 5, 6, 7, 14, 17, 21, 33, 34, 35, 36, 37, 42, 45, 51, 52, 59, 62, 65, 66, 74, 82, 85, 86, 88, 89, 90, 91, 100, 101, 105, 108, 110, 126, 130, 131, 134, 138, 141
financial condition, vii, 66, 74, 82, 85, 86, 90, 109, 110, 138
financial crisis, 105, 108
financial institutions, 37
financial reports, 52, 141
financial stability, 21, 101
First Class single-piece mail, 1
fiscal year (FY), 4, 5, 15, 26, 52, 54, 57, 96, 98, 100, 104, 108, 110, 111, 112,

117, 120, 124, 127, 128, 129, 130, 132, 138, 139, 140, 141, 142, 143, 144
five-day delivery, 2, 22, 25, 26, 47, 57
fixed costs, 20, 77
flexibility, 2, 16, 52, 76, 80
force, 19, 55, 66, 74, 82, 108, 116
formula, 12, 99
funding, 4, 41, 42, 54, 85, 86, 87, 88, 92, 93, 97
funds, 17, 61, 88, 95

G

General Accounting Office (GAO), 18, 20, 26, 28, 30, 55, 56, 58, 59, 74, 75, 76, 77, 82, 83, 94, 96, 100, 101, 103, 105, 106, 107, 111, 112, 114, 116, 119, 120, 128, 137, 140, 142, 143, 144
goods and services, 99
Great Recession, 51, 67, 81, 101
Gross Domestic Product, 128, 139, 143
growth, 1, 2, 9, 10, 12, 16, 25, 35, 73
guidance, 106, 107, 110, 122, 126, 130, 132, 133, 134, 135, 137, 138, 140, 144

H

health, 1, 3, 5, 6, 15, 16, 17, 41, 42, 54, 55, 71, 80, 81, 83, 86, 87, 88, 89, 90, 91, 92, 100, 101, 112, 126, 140, 141
health insurance, 17, 90, 92, 112
hiring, 18, 75, 80, 112
history, 57, 59, 100
hourly wage, 20, 56, 77
House, 2, 41, 42, 43, 44, 45, 46, 47, 48, 49, 59, 60, 62, 92, 97, 98, 100, 101, 102, 108
House of Representatives, 108
household income, 129
human resources, 18, 71
hybrid, 35

I

immigrants, 37
improvements, 97, 135
income, 4, 36, 90, 129
individuals, 36, 87, 93, 94, 97, 103
inflation, 91, 128
infrastructure, 133
institutions, 36, 37, 63
internal controls, 138
issues, vii, 1, 2, 3, 21, 24, 31, 54, 58, 83, 90, 93, 97, 102, 135

L

law enforcement, 103
laws, 95, 109, 137
layoffs, 19, 74
legislation, 2, 3, 17, 21, 34, 37, 50, 86, 97, 102
legislative proposals, 77, 97
life expectancy, 32
liquidate, 16, 88
loans, 5, 37

M

mail processing facilities, 2, 21, 24, 80
mail sorting facilities, vii, 85
majority, 16, 66, 68, 74, 101, 132, 139, 142, 143
management, 15, 59, 134, 137, 140, 144
manufacturing, 32
Market Dominant Products, 1, 7
market share, 33, 53
marketplace, 35
Medicare, 2, 41, 42, 86, 92
memorandums of understanding, 109, 118, 137
methodology, 13, 93, 95, 100, 110, 130, 138, 143
migration, 18, 75
mission, 31, 59, 109
models, 35, 62

modifications, 116, 143
morale, 31, 59
mortality, 97
multiple factors, 13

N

National Association of Postmasters of the United States (NAPUS), 108, 109, 110, 113, 118, 137, 138, 141
National League of Postmasters of the United States (NLPM), 108, 109, 110, 113, 118, 137, 138, 141
nonpostal products, 2, 3, 7, 33, 34, 37, 41, 42, 43, 45, 46, 51, 61
Non-Traditional Full-Time (NTFT), 55, 83, 108, 119, 120

O

Office of Management and Budget (OMB), 29, 100, 108, 110, 126, 135, 140, 143, 144
Office of the Inspector General, 54, 55, 56, 57, 62, 76, 83, 99
officials, 106, 107, 109, 110, 113, 114, 115, 116, 118, 120, 121, 124, 125, 127, 129, 130, 131, 137, 138, 139, 142, 143, 144
omission, 135
operating costs, vii, 85, 87, 112
operating revenue, 7, 9, 12, 17, 74
operating revenues, 74
operations, vii, 3, 4, 16, 21, 25, 27, 79, 80, 83, 85, 86, 87, 131, 132
opportunities, 35, 37, 116, 117, 135
oversight, 55, 82, 94, 100, 101, 107, 131, 134, 135, 137, 140
overtime, 19, 30, 76, 142, 144

P

part time post office (PTPO), 108, 114, 139
Part-Time Flexible (PTF), 108, 119, 120
pension funding, 41, 42, 54, 86, 87, 97
pension plans, 87
personnel costs, 15, 16, 30, 65, 66, 74
policy, 17, 28, 36, 55, 82, 87, 88, 89, 90, 92, 93, 97
population, 2, 36, 73, 129
population density, 129
population growth, 73
Post Office Structure Plan (POStPlan), 26, 55, 58, 105, 106, 107, 108, 109, 111, 113, 114, 115, 116, 117, 118, 119, 120, 121, 122, 123, 124, 125, 126, 127, 128, 129, 130, 131, 132, 133, 134, 135, 136, 137, 139, 140, 141, 142, 143, 144
post offices, 2, 26, 27, 33, 37, 105, 106, 107, 109, 110, 111, 113, 114, 115, 116, 117, 118, 119, 120, 121, 122, 123, 124, 125, 126, 127, 128, 129, 130, 131, 132, 133, 135, 136, 137, 138, 139, 140, 141, 142, 143, 144
postage, vii, 85, 87, 90
postal banking, 2, 34, 36, 37, 61
postal delivery standards, 2, 26
postal fleet, 2, 43, 46
Postal Inspection Service, 4, 79
postal products, vii, 3, 4, 7, 85
postal reform, vii, 1, 2, 34, 85, 87
Postal Regulatory Commission (PRC), 4, 5, 12, 13, 15, 20, 23, 24, 26, 27, 29, 40, 51, 52, 53, 54, 55, 56, 57, 58, 60, 61, 77, 78, 83, 91, 94, 95, 102, 103, 108, 109, 110, 122, 123, 126, 130, 131, 133, 137, 138, 140, 141, 142, 143, 144
postal service, 4, 6, 11, 21, 31, 33, 35, 36, 41, 42, 60, 86, 129, 130, 140
Postal Support Employee (PSE), 19, 55, 71, 72, 80, 82, 83, 84, 108, 112, 141
Postmaster Relief (PMR), 72, 81, 108, 126
private banks, 35, 37
private firms, 81
private sector, 33, 101

privatization, 99
profit, 4, 9, 26
protection, 44, 48, 49
public interest, 37
public sector, 33

R

recession, 12, 13, 53
recommendations, iv, 103, 106, 130, 133
reduction in force (RIF), 19, 55, 66, 74, 108, 116, 142
Reform, 1, 2, 3, 21, 25, 31, 34, 41, 42, 43, 44, 45, 46, 47, 48, 49, 51, 59, 60, 65, 66, 85, 87, 92, 93, 94, 98, 100, 101, 102, 108
regulations, 53, 109, 137
regulatory oversight, 140
reliability, 106, 107, 109, 110, 121, 122, 137, 140, 144
relief, 81, 91, 114, 119, 143
remotely managed post office (RMPO), 108, 114, 126, 128, 139
Reorganization Act, 2, 86, 93
requirements, 3, 16, 17, 32, 45, 46, 54, 86, 88, 92, 95, 100, 102, 103, 126, 130, 143
resolution, 3, 118, 136
resources, 18, 55, 71, 82, 107
response, 20, 77, 109, 127, 133, 134
restructuring, 55, 82, 108
retail, 2, 14, 21, 25, 26, 27, 30, 33, 47, 60, 78, 79, 80, 81, 105, 106, 107, 109, 111, 113, 114, 117, 121, 127, 129, 131, 132, 133, 140, 141, 144
retiree health benefits, 16, 86, 87, 88, 89, 90, 91, 92, 100, 101, 140, 141
retirement, 6, 17, 46, 55, 82, 83, 86, 87, 89, 90, 93, 94, 95, 97, 98, 100, 102, 104, 112, 142
revenue, 1, 3, 4, 7, 8, 9, 10, 11, 12, 13, 14, 17, 25, 26, 33, 35, 36, 37, 40, 52, 53, 62, 65, 66, 87, 90, 106, 107, 108, 110, 111, 121, 126, 127, 128, 129, 130, 131, 132, 133, 135, 139, 141, 143, 144
risk, 62, 74, 108, 122, 125, 134
rules, 56, 100, 113, 118, 134, 142
rural areas, 26, 73, 79

S

savings, 20, 24, 25, 26, 27, 36, 37, 61, 63, 105, 106, 107, 109, 110, 117, 119, 120, 121, 122, 123, 124, 125, 126, 129, 130, 131, 132, 133, 134, 135, 136, 137, 143
Secretary of the Treasury, 51
security, 58, 90, 101
self-sufficiency, 3
Senate, 2, 42, 43, 44, 47, 49, 50, 59, 92, 97, 98, 100, 102
sensitivity, 107, 110, 121, 125, 132, 133, 138, 140, 144
services, vii, 2, 3, 4, 7, 10, 13, 15, 16, 21, 25, 30, 31, 33, 34, 35, 36, 37, 40, 42, 43, 45, 46, 47, 51, 61, 62, 79, 85, 86, 87, 90, 99, 111, 113, 129, 130, 140, 143
staffing, 21, 31, 58, 76, 105, 106, 109, 113, 114, 116, 117, 118, 120, 121, 123, 125, 132, 136, 137, 138, 142, 143
stakeholders, 28, 77, 100, 106, 110, 121, 134, 137, 138, 141
state, 25, 35, 46, 60, 62, 84, 90,107, 122, 125, 126, 129, 133, 134, 135, 136
statutory authority, 5, 35
structural reforms, 3
structure, 3, 30, 141
supervision, 51
supervisors, 18, 75, 124, 142
support services, 113
surplus, 93, 96, 98, 101, 104
sustainability, 21, 65

T

target, 23, 86
taxpayers, 17, 87, 90
technical support, 80
time frame, 107, 130, 132
total revenue, 7, 14, 128
training, 25, 31, 33
transactions, 100, 133
transportation, 7, 15, 16, 24, 25, 33, 54, 60, 73, 81
Treasury, 4, 5, 16, 51, 61, 87, 95, 100, 108

U

U.S. Department of Labor, 6
U.S. Department of the Treasury, 51, 52
U.S. Postal Inspection Service, 4
U.S. Postal Inspection Service (USPIS), 4
U.S. Postal Service (USPS), v, vii, 1, 2, 3, 4, 5, 6, 7, 8, 9, 10, 11, 12, 13, 14, 15, 16, 17, 18, 19, 20, 21, 22, 23, 24, 25, 26, 27, 28, 29, 30, 31, 32, 33, 34, 35, 36, 37, 38, 40, 41, 42, 43, 44, 45, 47, 48, 49, 50, 51, 52, 53, 54, 55, 56, 57, 58, 59, 60, 61, 62, 65, 66,67, 68, 69, 70, 71, 72, 73, 74, 75, 76, 77, 78, 79, 80, 81, 82, 83, 84, 85, 86, 87, 88, 89, 90, 91, 92, 93, 94, 95, 96, 97, 98, 99, 100, 101, 102, 103, 104, 105, 106, 107, 108, 109, 111, 112, 113, 114, 115, 116, 117, 118, 119, 120, 121, 122, 123, 124, 125,126, 127, 128, 129, 130, 131, 132, 133, 134, 135, 136, 137, 139, 140, 141, 142, 143, 144
U.S. Treasury, 5, 16, 61, 87, 95, 100, 108
unions, 28, 30, 31, 71, 112
United Kingdom, 35, 61
United States, v, 2, 5, 15, 37, 42, 43, 44, 47, 48, 49, 51, 52, 53, 54, 55, 56, 57, 58, 59, 61, 79, 81, 83, 98, 102, 103, 105, 108, 109, 137
USPS post offices, vii, 85

V

vacancies, 116
variations, 122
vehicles, 31, 32, 80
Vice President, 59, 60
voters, 4, 87

W

wage rate, 19, 20, 56, 66
wages, 19, 31, 68, 76, 112, 142
Washington, 36, 51, 52, 54, 62, 79, 81, 100, 102, 140, 143, 144
windows, 30, 78
withdrawal, 97
workers, 14, 15, 54, 55, 83, 87, 95, 102, 103, 140, 141
workforce, vii, 1, 2, 14, 17, 19, 20, 25, 26, 28, 29, 30, 31, 55, 65, 66, 67, 68, 69, 74, 76, 77, 78, 79, 82, 83, 85, 91, 95, 96, 98, 100, 102, 104, 112
working conditions, 31, 142
workload, 25, 113, 114, 124, 126, 129, 132, 135, 141, 142
workplace, 58, 83